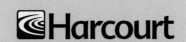
Harcourt

S0-AJF-950

PHONICS
Practice Book

Grade 2

Harcourt

Orlando   Boston   Dallas   Chicago   San Diego

Visit *The Learning Site!*
www.harcourtschool.com

Toronto   London

ISBN 0-15-315212-5

23 24 25 26 073 10 09 08 07

CONTENTS

Unit 1: Consonants and Short Vowels

Unit 2: Long Vowels

Unit 3: More Work with Vowels

Unit 4: Consonant Clusters

Unit 5: Consonant Digraphs

Unit 6: Possessives and Contractions

Unit 7: Inflected Endings and Suffixes

Cut-Out Fold-Up Books:

Phonics Practice Book

Say each picture name. Circle and write the letter that stands for the beginning sound. Then color the picture.

1	m c b	
2	p j l	
3	p t v	

4	d s m	
5	w r z	
6	k f y	

7	b n h	
8	b z j	
9	l h r	

10	z d r	
11	d v s	
12	k l v	

Name _____

Say each picture name. Circle and write the letter that stands for the beginning sound. Then color the picture.

1 p j y	2 f r n	3 p k w
4 z t v	5 b f s	6 m g h
7 d r m	8 p x j	9 r l g
10 t z f	11 c h d	12 n v w

Harcourt Brace School Publishers

Name _____

Write the picture names to complete the puzzle.

sun	dog	top	web	rock
bus	pig	mask	cat	yarn

Name _____

Say each picture name. Write the letter that stands for the beginning sound. Then trace the whole word.

1	2	3
___ an	___ en	___ et

4	5	6
___ ebra	___ oll	___ oat

7	8	9
___ eaf	___ ix	___ and

10	11	12
___ et	___ ite	___ oon

Say each picture name. Write the letter that stands for the beginning sound. Then trace the whole word.

1	2	3
ap	ake	ox

4	5	6
ape	arn	ed

7	8	9
ot	op	est

10	11	12
at	ar	ell

Name _____

Circle the name of each picture. Then write the word on the line.

1	tack back sack	2	hop pop top	3	jog fog log
4	fan pan man	5	sand hand band	6	big dig pig
7	kit sit hit	8	wet get net	9	goat boat coat
10	rock dock sock	11	zip tip rip	12	bug rug tug

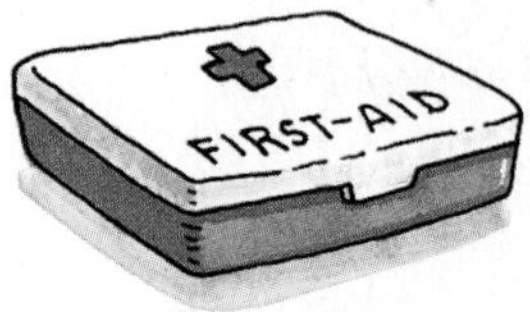

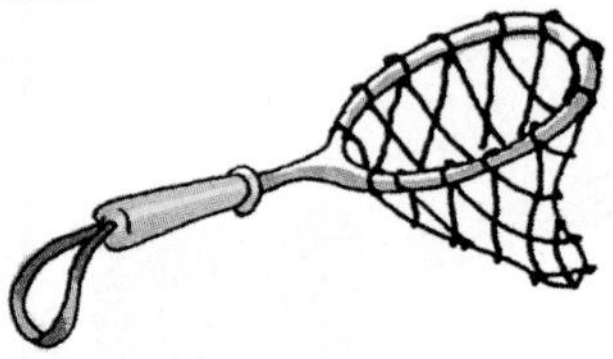

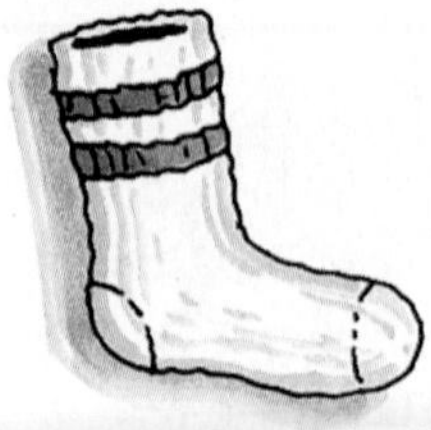

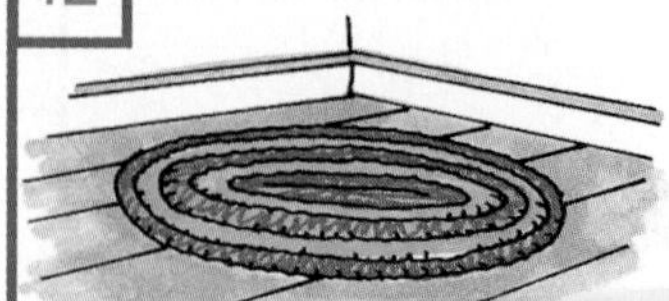

Initial Consonants • Reading Words

Phonics Practice Book

Name _____

Say each picture name. Circle and write the letter or letters that stand for the ending sound. Then color the picture.

1	p m f	2	g x n	3	t f l
4	n d z	5	f g k	6	t l x
7	t l p	8	ll ff ss	9	r l m
10	m f t	11	dd gg zz	12	d l s

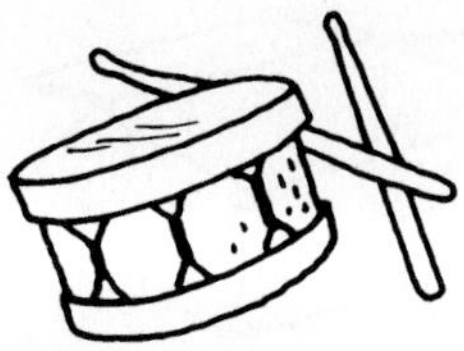

Final Consonants **13**

Name _____

Say each picture name. Circle and write the letter or letters that stand for the ending sound. Then color the picture.

1		g
		b
		k

_____

2		tt
		ss
		gg

_____

3		n
		r
		s

_____

4		ll
		zz
		ff

_____

5		r
		b
		k

_____

6		r
		l
		n

_____

7		dd
		gg
		ff

_____

8		b
		f
		s

_____

9		k
		p
		l

_____

10		n
		g
		f

_____

11		m
		g
		s

_____

12		z
		r
		x

_____

Harcourt Brace School Publishers

Look at the pictures. Then write the picture names to complete the puzzles.

pot	dog	drum	dress
tail	toad	pin	door

Final Consonants: Reading Words

Say each picture name. Write the letter that stands for the ending sound. Then trace the whole word.

1	2	3
___ boo	___ bu	___ bi

4	5	6
___ lea	___ ca	___ ca

7	8	9
___ a	___ nu	___ be

10	11	12
___ pe	___ nai	___ gu

Say each picture name. Write the letter that stands for the ending sound. Then trace the whole word.

1	2	3
cu___	bu___	plu___

4	5	6
te___	hu___	bea___

7	8	9
tai___	boa___	cra___

10	11	12
li___	fo___	bea___

Name _____

Circle the name of each picture. Then write the picture name on the line.

1 	rod rot rob	2 	car can cat	3 	cot cob cod
4 	fat fad fan	5	pop pot pod	6 	been boat beak
7 	mitt mill miss	8 	seat seal seam	9 	bet bell buzz
10 	leg let led	11 	leaf let look	12 	pit pin pig

Final Consonants

Phonics Practice Book

Name _____

Say each picture name. Write the letter that stands for the middle sound. Then trace the whole word.

1	2	3
le __ on	sha __ ow	ti __ er

4	5	6
ca __ in	pa __ er	tu __ ip

7	8	9
mo __ ey	be __ ide	pe __ al

10	11	12
ro __ ot	ru __ er	wa __ on

Name _____

Look at the pictures. Write the letter that stands for the sound in the middle of each picture name. Then trace the whole word.

Across

3

5

6

9

Down

1

2

4

8

7

3

Crossword grid letters:

1 b

2 p o e y

3 s h a o w

s a y a

d r a o n

i u

e i

r a

9 r o i n

Medial Consonants

Phonics Practice Book

Name _____

Write the word that makes each sentence tell about the picture.

| daddy | puppy | bubbles |
| silly | kitten | ladder |

1.

I watched some _____ fly up high.

2.

A _____ ran into the garden.

3.

My _____ climbed up onto a branch.

4.

I shouted for my _____ to get my cat.

5.

He climbed a _____ to get my cat.

6.

Now my _____ cat and the dog are playing together!

Medial Consonants

Name_____

1. Make Bee a queen. Put a crown on her head.

2. Which animal is winning because it is very quick? Color it blue.

3. Find the quiet animal that is reading. Color it green.

4. Make a quilt. Put it next to Pig.

5. What animal says "quack"? Put an **X** on it.

6. Give Pony a quarter. Put it on Pony's back.

Name _____

quick   quilt   quack   quiet   queen   quit

THE KING'S SURPRISE

The king wanted to surprise the _____ for her

birthday. He went to his friend Duck for help. "What can I

give her?" the king asked.

Duck was _____ for a while. Then he said, "She

might like a nice _____."

"You're right," the king said. "I will make her one. I will

get started now. I must be _____! I will not

_____ until I'm done."

"When is her birthday?" Duck asked with a _____.

"Today!" shouted the king.

"Good luck," said Duck.

Name _____

Say each picture name. Write the letter that completes the word. Then trace the whole word.

1 pa __ er	2 __ uck	3 fo __
4 fa __	5 ro __ ot	6 __ at
7 ru __ er	8 __ oon	9 bu __
10 __ et	11 pi __	12 le __ on

Review of Initial, Medial, and Final Consonants

Phonics Practice Book

Harcourt Brace School Publishers

Name _____

Say each picture name. Write the letter that completes the word.
Then trace the whole word.

1 ____ pi ____	2 ti ____ er	3 ____ at
4 sha ____ ow	5 lea ____	6 pe ____ al
7 ____ ell	8 doo ____	9 mo ____ ey
10 ____ an	11 ____ am	12 nai ____

CHECK-UP

Fill in the circle next to the letter or letters that complete the word. Write the letter or letters. Then trace the whole word.

1
○ f
○ g
○ s

___ish___

2
○ ss
○ ll
○ gg

___dre___

3
○ ll
○ zz
○ tt

___ki___en___

4
○ m
○ b
○ g

___tu___

5
○ m
○ l
○ t

___ion___

6
○ p
○ t
○ m

___dru___

7
○ dd
○ pp
○ bb

___la___er___

8
○ x
○ s
○ t

___be___ide___

9
○ t
○ g
○ m

___ouse___

10
○ s
○ d
○ l

___tu___ip___

11
○ qu
○ x
○ y

___ilt___

12
○ dd
○ gg
○ ll

___e___

Harcourt Brace School Publishers

Name _____

Fill in the circle next to the letter or letters that complete the word. Write the letter or letters. Then trace the whole word.

✓ CHECK-UP

1.
○ dd
○ ll
○ tt

mi ___

2.
○ g
○ f
○ d

___ oat

3.
○ r
○ p
○ m

le ___ on

4.
○ dd
○ ll
○ zz

pi ___ ow

5.
○ f
○ d
○ k

be ___

6.
○ m
○ w
○ s

___ un

7.
○ w
○ m
○ d

___ agon

8.
○ n
○ g
○ b

ba ___ y

9.
○ r
○ s
○ p

cu ___

10.
○ tt
○ pp
○ ll

be ___

11.
○ bb
○ zz
○ ll

ra ___ it

12.
○ b
○ l
○ y

___ arn

Harcourt Brace School Publishers

The word **fox** has the short **o** sound. Write **o** to complete each picture name that has the short **o** sound. Then trace the whole word.

f**o**x

1	2	3
t __ p	p __ t	h __ p

4	5	6
h __ t	n __ t	d __ ll

7	8	9
c __ t	b __ x	__ l __ ck

10	11	12
sp __ t	s __ x	m __ p

Harcourt Brace School Publishers

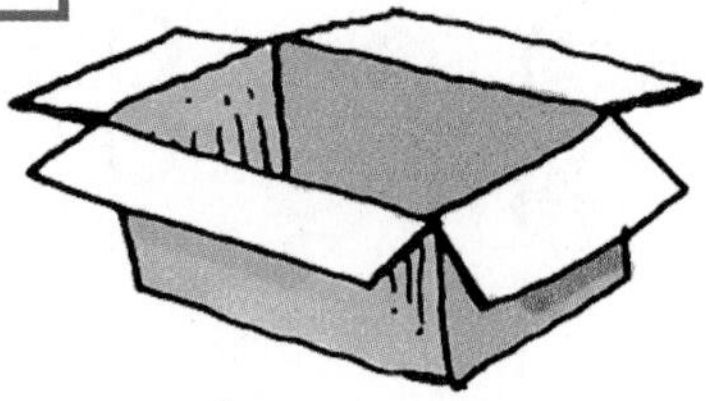

Short Vowel: / o / o

Phonics Practice Book

Look at each picture. Then write its name on the line.

1	2	3
_____	_____	_____

4	5	6
_____	_____	_____

7	8	9
_____	_____	_____

The picture names in each row rhyme. Write the picture names. Then write a word that rhymes with the picture names. Draw a picture for your word.

p<u>o</u>p

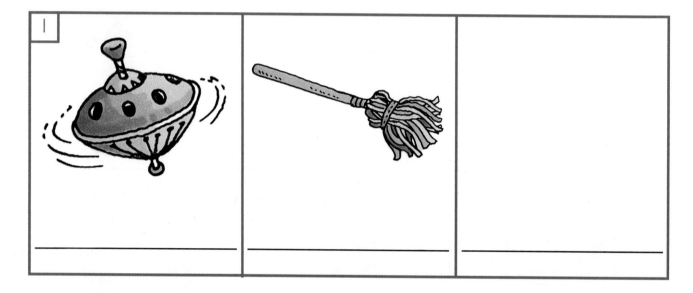

h<u>o</u>t

Harcourt Brace School Publishers

Name_____

Read the poem. Then complete the sentences.

Little Plants

We find a pot.

We plant a lot.

The days get very, very hot!

Soon up plants pop.

I see leaves on top.

Grow, little plants! Don't stop!

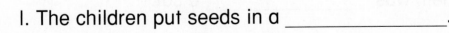

1. The children put seeds in a _____.

2. The plants _____ up.

3. They grow when the days are _____.

4. The leaves are on the _____.

Name_____

Write the word that completes each sentence.

box   on   shop   stop
spot   got   top   dolls

1. "Look in the window of this _____," said Todd.

2. "What has it _____ in it?" asked Bev.

3. "Let's _____ and look," said Todd.

4. Bev and Todd saw two _____.

5. One of them was _____ a cot.

6. The other was in a _____.

7. Bev saw a _____ that was turning around.

8. It was going around and around on the very same

_____!

Short Vowel: / o / o • Reading Words with Short o   Phonics Practice Book

Name _____

hen

The word **hen** has the short **e** sound. Write **e** to complete each picture name that has the short **e** sound. Then trace the whole word.

1 t n	2 b d	3 n t
4 m n	5 p n	6 w b
7 b ll	8 n t	9 sh ll
10 b ll	11 l g	12 n st

Look at the pictures. Write the picture names to complete the puzzles.

Short Vowel: / e / e • Writing Words with Short e

Harcourt Brace School Publishers

Phonics Practice Book

Name_____

The picture names in each row rhyme. Write the rhyming words.
Then write another rhyming word. Draw a picture for it.

 w**et**

1 		
_____	_____	_____

 m**en**

2		
_____	_____	_____

Short Vowel: / e / e • Phonograms

35

Name_____

Write the word that completes each sentence.

ten	pen	eggs
get	pets	red

1. Ben got two animals for _____ .

2. What did he _____?

3. He got one dog and one big _____ hen.

4. The hen lives in a _____ .

5. Look at the _____ in the hen's house.

6. Can you find all _____ of them?

Short Vowe: / e / e • Reading Words with Short *e*   Phonics Practice Book

Read the sentences and follow the directions.

1. Look for the jet. Color it red.

2. Meg has a pet. Make a box around it.

3. Find the bell. Color it blue.

4. Do you see a hen? Put an egg next to her.

5. Find the stem. Color it green.

6. Do you see the step? Put an **X** on it.

7. Find a net. Put a big fly in it.

8. Find two men with a TV set. Color them.

Name _____

Write **o** or **e** to complete each picture name. Then trace the whole word.

1 f __ x	2 cl __ ck	3 w __ b
4 p __ t	5 sl __ d	6 c __ t
7 n __ t	8 m __ p	9 b __ ll
10 t __ n	11 s __ cks	12 b __ d

Review of Short Vowels: / o / o, / e / e

Harcourt Brace School Publishers

Phonics Practice Book

Read the poem. Then answer the question.

The Hen and the Fox

One morning a pretty little hen

Was sitting on some rocks.

When who do you think came by at ten?

A very happy fox!

"What do you think I have," Fox said,

"Right inside this pot?

It is not blue or green or red.

But it is very hot!"

Just then the hen did hear a pop

And pop, Pop, POP, POP, POP!

Some food came flying from the top,

And did not ever stop!

What do you think was inside the pot?_____
Draw a picture of it.

The word **cat** has the short **a** sound. Write **a** to complete each picture name that has the short **a** sound. Then trace the whole word.

c**a**t

1	2	3
fl__g	c__n	m__p
4	5	6
b__d	b__t	m__p
7	8	9
c__p	p__n	b__g
10	11	12
m__n	s__cks	f__n

Name_____

Look at the pictures. Write the picture names to complete the puzzles.

Short Vowel: / a / *a*: Writing Words with Short *a*

Name_____

The picture names in each row rhyme. Write the rhyming words.
Then write another rhyming word and draw a picture for it.

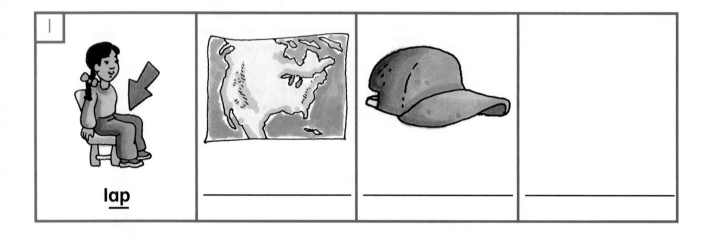

1

lap _____ _____ _____

2

van _____ _____ _____

3

mat _____ _____ _____

Short Vowel: / a / a • Phonograms

Phonics Practice Book

Write the word that makes each sentence tell about the picture.

| cat | asked | as | and | sat | can't |

1. Sam _____ find his cat.

2. He _____ Pam to help.

3. Sam _____ Pam looked in the yard.

4. The _____ was not in the grass.

5. Sam saw a hat that was as big _____ a sack.

6. The cat _____ in the big hat.

Short Vowel: / a / a • Reading Words with Short a

Name _____

Write the word from the box that completes each sentence.

sad	sat	tag	am
dad	as	had	ran

1. Pam _____ at the table with her friends.

2. She _____ a big birthday cake.

3. Her _____ made it for her.

4. Pam said, "Today is great. I _____ glad."

5. Gran said, "Everybody is happy. Nobody is_____."

6. Pam's friend Max asked, "Can we play_____?"

7. All her friends got up and _____.

8. Pam shouted, "Run _____ fast as you can!"

Short Vowel: / a / a • Reading Words with Short a

The word **pig** has the short **i** sound. Write **i** to complete each picture name that has the short **i** sound. Then trace the whole word.

p_ig

1	2	3
p _ g	p _ n	cr _ b

4	5	6
b _ b	b _ d	w _ g

7	8	9
s _ x	cl _ p	p _ n

10	11	12
l _ d	b _ t	f _ n

Name _____

Look at the pictures. Write the pictures' names to complete the puzzles.

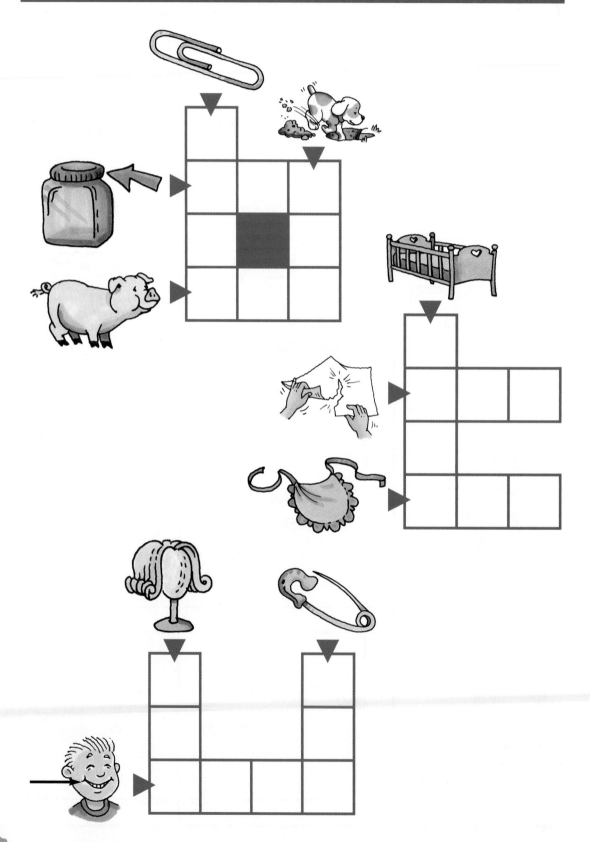

Short Vowel: / i / i • Writing Words with Short i

Phonics Practice Book

Harcourt Brace School Publishers

Name _____

The picture names in each row rhyme. Write the rhyming words.
Then write another rhyming word and draw a picture for it.

1. <u>win</u>

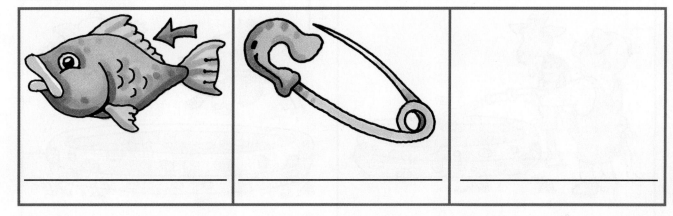

_____ _____ _____

2. b<u>ig</u>

_____ _____ _____

3. s<u>ip</u>

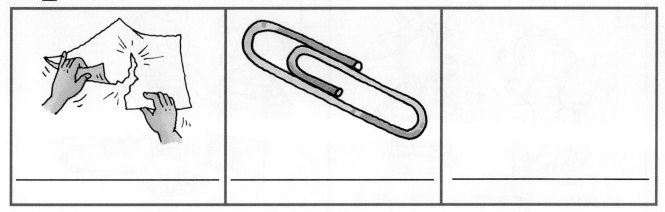

_____ _____ _____

Short Vowel: / i / i • Phonograms

Name_____

mix   fill   hit   in   fix   flip

1

Let's _____ it up.

2

Now let's go _____.

3

We have to _____ this.

4

I will _____ it.

5

I will _____ it.

6

Then I will _____ it.

Short Vowel: / i / i • Reading Words with Short i

Phonics Practice Book

Name_____

Write the word that completes each sentence.

mitt	six	will	did
hit	grin	win	is

1. Did you see the good _____ Rick got with his bat?

2. I think Kim will make the catch with her _____.

3. Kim made _____ great catches today!

4. Look at the happy _____ on Kim's face.

5. Kim _____ make a great catch!

6. Now it _____ Kim's turn to bat.

7. Maybe she _____ get a home run!

8. Who do you think will _____?

Harcourt Brace School Publishers

Write **a** or **i** to complete each picture name. Then trace the whole word.

1	2	3
p n	f n	w g

4	5	6
m p	h nd	h t

7	8	9
cl p	p th	cr b

10	11	12
m t	s x	p g

Review of Short Vowels: / a / *a*, / i / *i*

Phonics Practice Book

Harcourt Brace School Publishers

Name _____

Circle the sentence that tells about the picture.

1		The pig has a cap. The pig's friend is a cat. Pig gave cat a cap.
2		Cat sat with me. Cat is kicking it. Cat taps on it.
3		Look at the sheep grin. The sheep sits and claps. A sheep is in a bag.
4		Dog digs with that. Dog dances a fast jig. Dog has a red bib.
5		The bat is in a band. The bat slid down the hill. The bat has six hats.
6		The duck sits in a crib. That wig is on a fat pig. The wig is on the duck.

Harcourt Brace School Publishers

nut

The word **nut** has the short **u** sound. Write **u** to complete each picture name that has the short **u** sound. Then trace the whole word.

1	c b	2	f n	3	g m
4	d ck	5	h g	6	c b
7	b g	8	t b	9	s n
10	j mp	11	b d	12	dr m

Look at the pictures. Write the picture names to complete the puzzles.

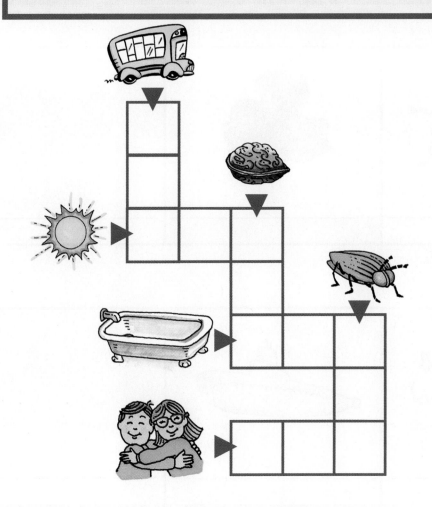

Short Vowel: / u / u • Writing Words with Short *u*

53

The picture names in each row rhyme. Write the rhyming words.
Then write another rhyming word. Draw a picture for it.

jug

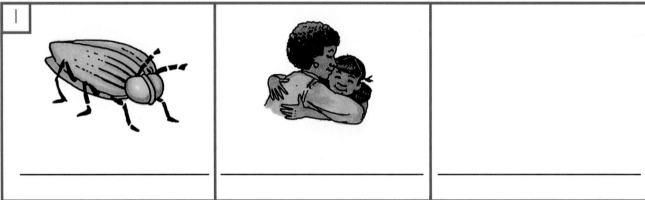

1 | | |
_____ | _____ | _____

rub

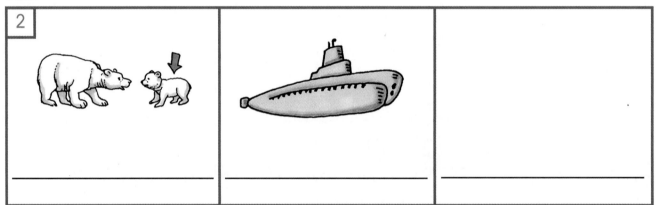

2 | | |
_____ | _____ | _____

nut

3 | | |
_____ | _____ | _____

Harcourt Brace School Publishers

Do what the sentences tell you.

1. Find the pup. Give it a drum.

2. Where is the bug? Color it red.

3. Put a cup on top of the duck.

4. Make the skunk black and white.

5. The animals jump in the mud. Color the mud blue.

6. Put a face on the sun.

7. Put a cub up in the tree.

8. The animals must go home. Put them in the tub to scrub.

Name _____

Write the word that completes each riddle.

fun	bug	rug	mug
skunk	bus	drum	jump

1. It is small. It can fly. It is a _____.

2. You have this when you have a good time.

   You have _____.

3. It has four feet. Keep away from it! It is a _____.

4. You do this with your feet. You _____.

5. Some children ride this to school. It is a _____.

6. It can go rat-a-tat-tat. It is a _____.

7. It is something you drink from. It is a _____.

8. It is like a mat. It is a _____.

Short Vowel: / u / u • Reading words with Short u

Name _____

Circle the letter that stands for the vowel sound in each picture name. Then write the word.

SUPER REVIEW

1	a e i o u	2	a e i o u	3	a e i o u
_____		_____		_____	

4	a e i o u	5	a e i o u	6	a e i o u
_____		_____		_____	

7	a e i o u	8	a e i o u	9	a e i o u
_____		_____		_____	

10	a e i o u	11	a e i o u	12	a e i o u
_____		_____		_____	

Circle the letter that stands for the vowel sound in each picture name. Then write the word.

1	a e i o u	2	a e i o u	3	a e i o u
_____		_____		_____	

4	a e i o u	5	a e i o u	6	a e i o u
_____		_____		_____	

7	a e i o u	8	a e i o u	9	a e i o u
_____		_____		_____	

10	a e i o u	11	a e i o u	12	a e i o u
_____		_____		_____	

Cumulative Review: Short Vowels • Writing Words with Short Vowels   Phonics Practice Book

Fill in the circle next to the name of each picture.

1
- ○ pop
- ○ pep
- ○ pup

2
- ○ bad
- ○ bed
- ○ bid

3
- ○ bag
- ○ big
- ○ bug

4
- ○ cat
- ○ cot
- ○ cut

5
- ○ him
- ○ hem
- ○ ham

6
- ○ track
- ○ trick
- ○ truck

7
- ○ fun
- ○ fin
- ○ fan

8
- ○ stack
- ○ stuck
- ○ stick

9
- ○ not
- ○ nut
- ○ net

10
- ○ pat
- ○ pot
- ○ pet

11
- ○ sick
- ○ sock
- ○ sack

12
- ○ duck
- ○ deck
- ○ dock

Circle the sentence that tells about the picture.

1		If I hop, I will win. Frogs can hop. I like to pet my dog.
2		Meg puts it on the track. Meg will get her truck. Meg will do a trick.
3		She steps on the mat. She sits on the mat. She gets her mitt.
4		Sam gives a ride to a cub. Sam will ride in a cab. Sam likes to ride with a cat.
5		Give the pup a blue cap. Let the pup have a sip. Take the pup to the den.
6		There is a hen with my cat. There is a cat in the tent. There is a cat on my bed.

Harcourt Brace School Publishers

Name _____

Harcourt Brace School Publishers

The letters **ea** can stand for the short **e** sound. Write **ea** to complete each picture name that has the short **e** sound. Then trace the whole word.

h<u>ea</u>d

1. br___d

2. l___d

3. thr___d

4. f___ther

5. h___d

6. sk___nk

7. br___kfast

8. w___ther

9. ch___r

10. sw___ter

11. fl___er

12. spr___d

Short Vowel: / e / *ea*

Name _____

Circle the sentence that tells about the picture.

1	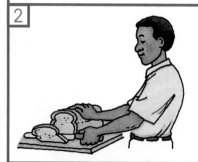	My cap is on my head. My cap is in my hand. I put my hand on my head.
2		He sees a pretty bud. He gets some books. He cuts the bread.
3		She sends the boy to bed. She puts a spread on the bed. She puts the jam on the bread.
4		It is so cold that I can see my breath. I am going to take a bath. Both of us like to play outside.
5		My father fed the hen. A frog hops to a feather. A feather fell from the hen.

Short Vowel: / e / ea

touch

Write the word that makes each sentence tell about the picture.

enough	cousin	rough
touched	country	tough

1. My _____ Julio is visiting me.

2. He comes from another _____.

3. Adios! Sometimes it is _____ to know what he is saying.

4. Today we found a rock that was very _____.

5. When I _____ it, I got a small cut!

6. Julio and I never have _____ time to do all that we want.

Name _____

Read the story and think about what happens. Write a short **u** word to complete each sentence about the story.

Doug's Horse Ride

Doug went to the farm to visit his cousin Pam. Pam took him to see her pets. She let him touch her horse. "His name is Tough," Pam said.

Then Doug climbed onto Tough. He said, "Tough feels rough!"

Pam asked, "Have you had enough?"

"Yes!" said Doug, and he got down.

They had a good laugh about his ride on Tough!

1. Pam's _____ is Doug.

2. Pam let Doug _____ her horse.

3. The horse felt _____.

4. Why do you think that Doug had _____?

5. Pam named her horse _____.

Harcourt Brace School Publishers

Name _____

Look at the first picture in each row. Circle and color the picture whose name rhymes with it.

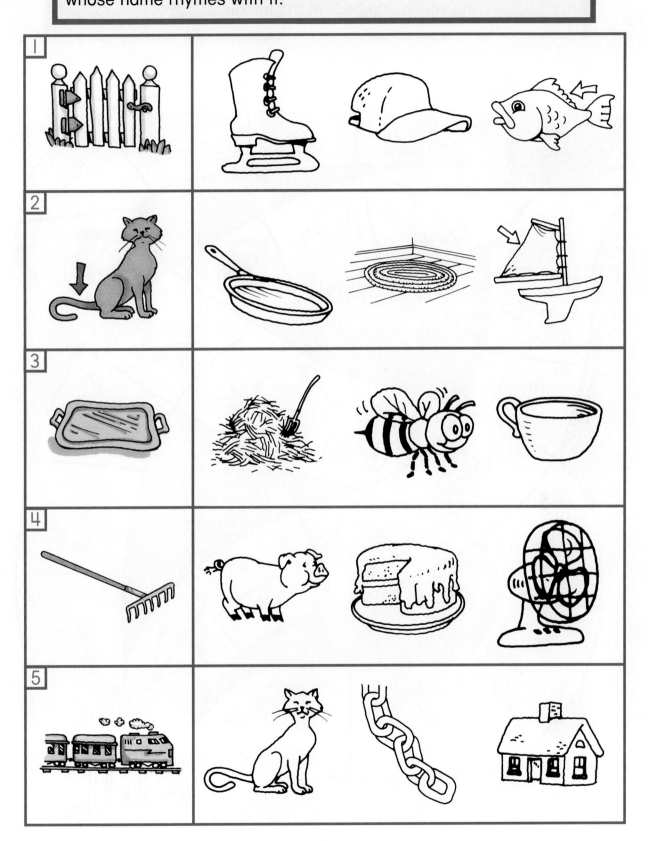

Harcourt Brace School Publishers

Long Vowel: / ā / • Phonemic Awareness

Name _____

Help the  find its way to the ▥. Color the pictures whose names have the sound you hear in the middle of 🐍 .

Long Vowel: / ā / • Phonemic Awareness

Phonics Practice Book

train

The letters **ai** can stand for the long **a** sound. Write **ai** to complete each picture name that has the long **a** sound. Then trace the whole word.

1	2	3
n___l	r___n	t___d

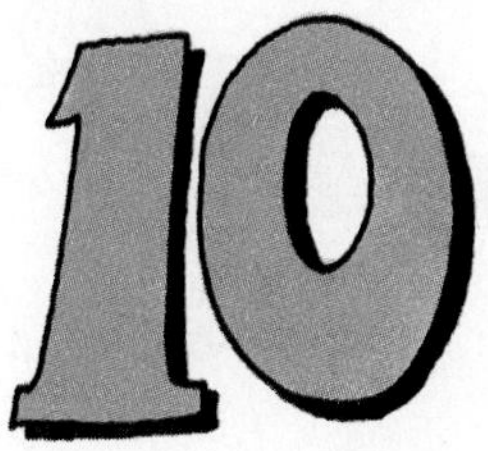

4	5	6
p___l	t___n	ch___n

7	8	9
r___d	dr___n	s___l

10	11	12
br___d	p___n	sn___l

Long Vowel: /ā/ *ai, ay, a-e*

Name _____

play

The letters **ay** can stand for the long **a** sound. Write **ay** to complete each picture name that has the long **a** sound. Then trace the whole word.

1. tr___

2. t___

3. h___

4. b___

5. j___

6. gr___

7. p___

8. pl___

9. r___

10. d___

11. tr___

12. p___

68

Long Vowel: / ā / ai, ay, a-e

Phonics Practice Book

Harcourt Brace School Publishers

Name _____

cake

The letters **a - e** can stand for the long **a** sound. Write the letters **a - e** to complete each picture name that has the long **a** sound. Then trace the whole word.

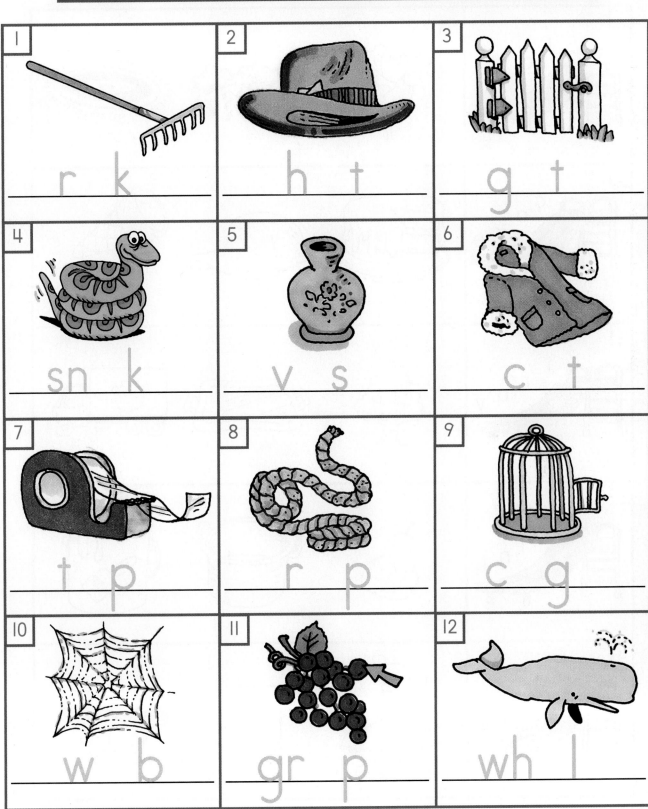

1. r__k
2. h__t
3. g__t
4. sn__k
5. v__s
6. c__t
7. t__p
8. r__p
9. c__g
10. w__b
11. gr__p
12. wh__l

Long Vowel: / ā / ai, ay, a-e

Slide and read the word. Circle and color the picture it names.

1. r a i n

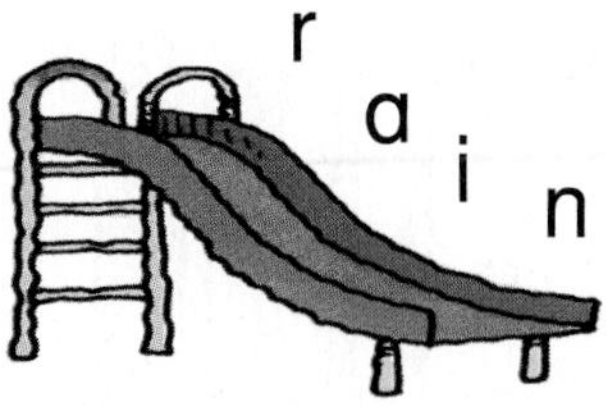

2. 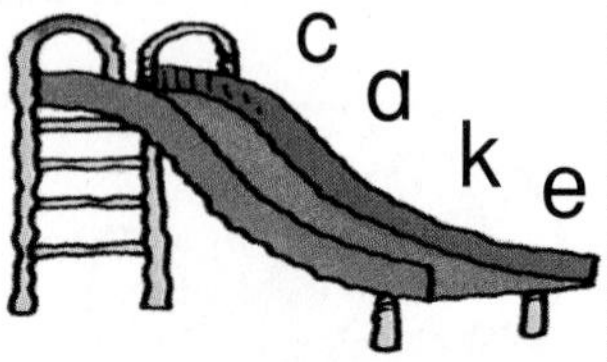 c a k e

3. 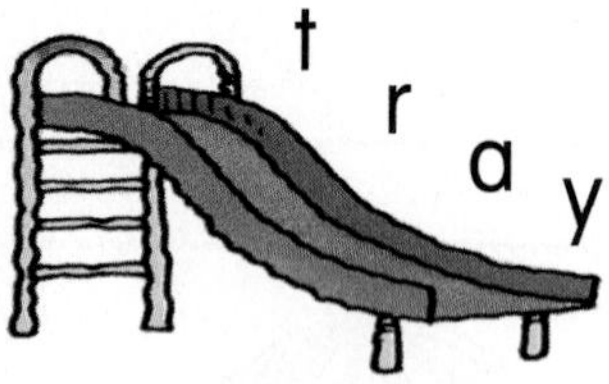 t r a y

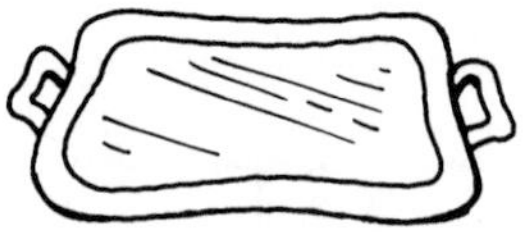

4. 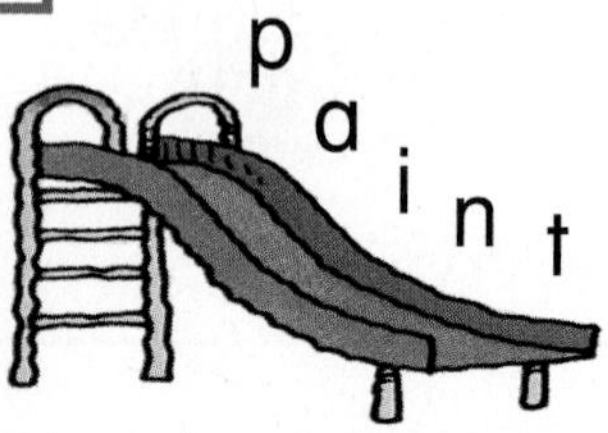 p a i n t

5. s k a t e

Long Vowel: / ā / ai, ay, a-e • Blending

Phonics Practice Book

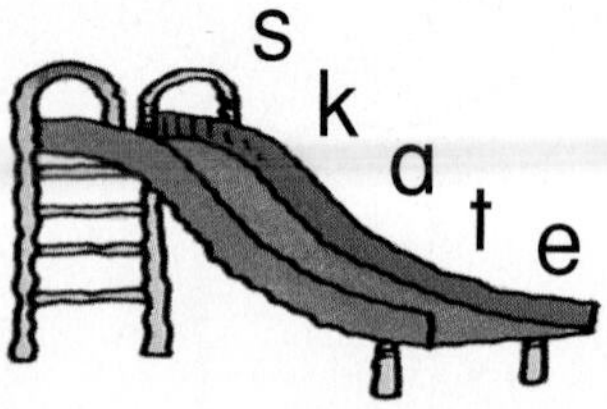

Harcourt Brace School Publishers

The picture names in each row rhyme. Write the rhyming words. Then write another rhyming word. Draw a picture for it.

1

h<u>ay</u>

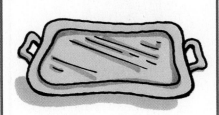

_____

_____

_____

2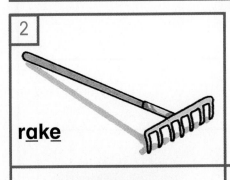

r<u>a</u>k<u>e</u>

_____

_____

_____

The **ai** in **tail,** the **a-e** in **cake,** and the **ay** in **ray** can all stand for the long **a** sound. Write the words where they belong in the chart. Then draw a picture for the last word in each column.

plane	hay	chain	snail
rain	vase	gate	gray
tray	pail	jay	cane

tail	cake	ray

Harcourt Brace School Publishers

Name _____

Circle and write the word that best completes each sentence.

1. Mother, ___
   we shop in here?   _____   may   me   my

2. We need a ___
   for the leaves.   _____   rock   rich   rake

3. I would like a ___
   to lock my bike.   _____   chain   chin   cane

4. Look at this pretty
   clay___.   _____   sick   snake   snack

5. Our mouse needs
   a nice ___.   _____   came   chug   cage

6. Do you see the
   ___ on the tracks?   _____   tan   trot   train

7. It would be fun to
   ___with that.   _____   plan   play   please

8. This small boat has
   a blue ___.   _____   sail   sell   sat

9. I will get the rose
   in this ___.   _____   vase   very   vane

10. Before we go, I must
    ___ for it.   _____   pay   pony   pat

Name _____

Circle 13 long **a** words hidden in the puzzle. Some words go across. Some words go down.

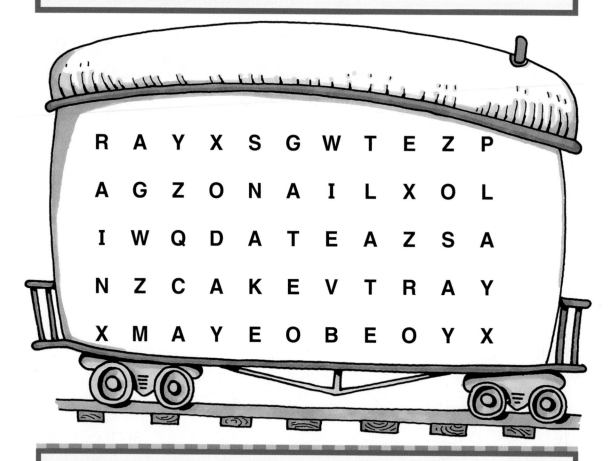

R A Y X S G W T E Z P
A G Z O N A I L X O L
I W Q D A T E A Z S A
N Z C A K E V T R A Y
X M A Y E O B E O Y X

Write the word from the puzzle that names each picture.

1. _____

2. _____

3. _____

4. _____

5. _____

6. _____

7. _____

8. _____

Long Vowel: / ā / *ai, ay, a-e* • Reading Words with Long *a*

Harcourt Brace School Publishers

Phonics Practice Book

Name _____

Circle the long **a** word in each question, and write it on the line.
Then circle the answer to each question.

1. Can a pet bird be in a cage? _____   Yes   No

2. Is a flame very cold? _____   Yes   No

3. Can you eat cake? _____   Yes   No

4. Can you put water in a pail? _____   Yes   No

5. Is a red dress gray? _____   Yes   No

6. Can you eat a grape? _____   Yes   No

7. Do snails dance? _____   Yes   No

8. Can you get wet in the rain? _____   Yes   No

9. Can you run in a race? _____   Yes   No

10. Does a whale walk? _____   Yes   No

11. Can you see the sun on some days? _____   Yes   No

12. Can a cat say what you do? _____   Yes   No

Name _____

Sailing

Jay and Kate sometimes sail on the bay with their mother and father. The children put on life vests to stay safe.
Sometimes there are big waves in the water. Other times the water is as still as a lake.

"Today we would like to see a big gray whale," say Kate and Jay. "If we had our way, we would go out in the boat every day."

Write the long **a** word from the story that completes each sentence.

1. Jay and Kate like to _____.

2. They are in a boat on the _____.

3. Life vests help the children _____ safe.

4. Do you think a gray _____ lives in the water?

5. The children wish they could sail every _____.

Harcourt Brace School Publishers

Say the name of the picture in the box. Circle the picture whose name rhymes with it.

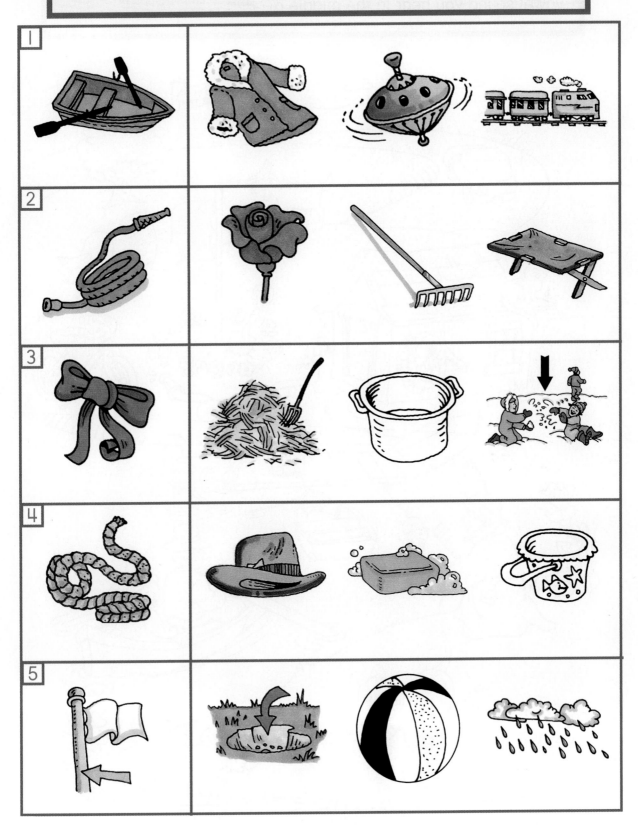

Long Vowel: / ō / • Phonemic Awareness

Joan is on a  . Color the pictures whose names have the vowel sound you hear in the middle of ▰ .

go

The letter **o** can stand for the long **o** sound. Write the letter **o** to complete each picture name that has the long **o** sound. Then trace the whole word.

1	2	3
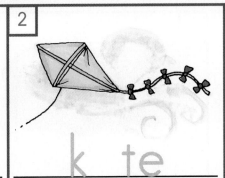 c __ ld	k __ te	r __ ll
4	5	6
 radi __	c __ t	c __ mb
7	8	9
f __ ld	wh __ le	c __ lt
10	11	12
 pian __	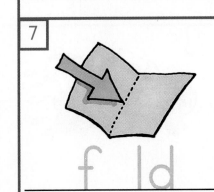 g __ ld	 h __ p

Long Vowel: / ō / o, oa

79

The letters **oa** often stand for the long **o** sound. Write **oa** to complete each picture name that has the long **o** sound. Then trace the whole word.

bo**a**t

1	2	3
c ___ t	r ___ d	c ___ t
4	**5**	**6**
s ___ p	g ___ t	t ___ p
7	**8**	**9**
t ___ d	c ___ n	s ___ k
10	**11**	**12**
r ___ n	c ___ ch	fl ___ t

Long Vowel: / ō / oa

Phonics Practice Book

Name _____

rope

The letters **o-e** often stand for the long **o** sound. Write the letters **o-e** to complete each picture name that has the long **o** sound. Then trace the whole word.

1	2	3
r___s	n___t	c___n

4	5	6
p___t	sm___k	p___l

7	8	9
h___l	c___k	h___s

10	11	12
b___n	g___t	r___b

The letters **ow** can stand for the long **o** sound. Write the letters **ow** to complete each picture name that has the long **o** sound. Then trace the whole word.

b<u>ow</u>

1 sn___	2 r___	3 tr___
4 m___	5 tr___	6 cr___
7 r___	8 sh___	9 bl___
10 gr___	11 kn___	12 thr___

Long Vowel: / ō / o-e, ow

Harcourt Brace School Publishers

Phonics Practice Book

Slide and read the word. Circle and color the picture it names.

1. s o a p

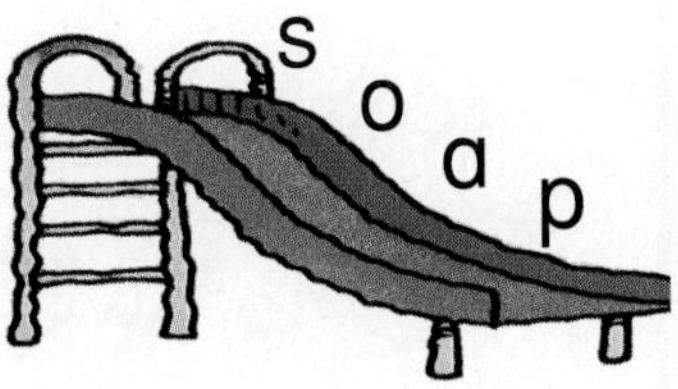

2. r o s e

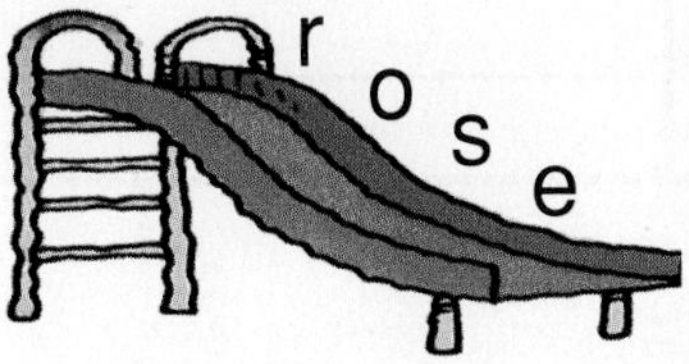

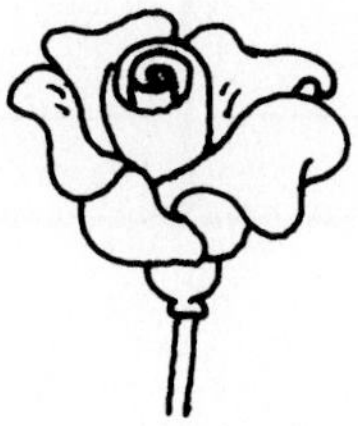

3. s n o w

4. g o l d

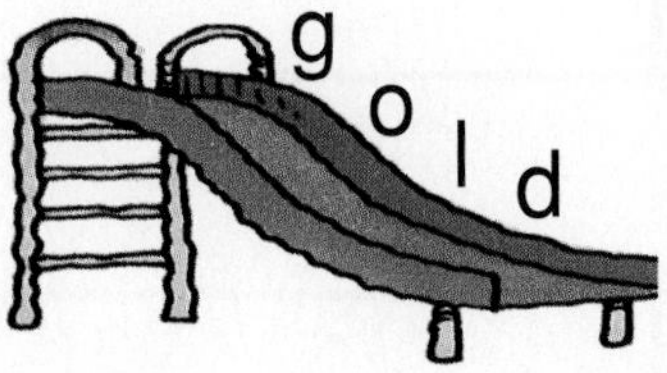

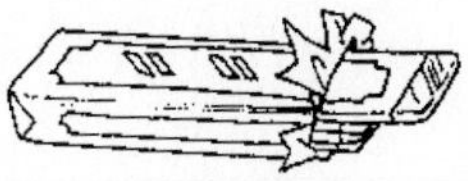

5. b o a t

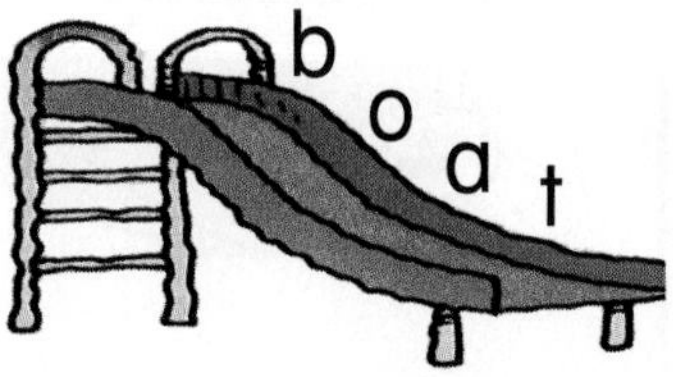

Long Vowel: / ō / o, oa, o-e, ow • Blending

Name _____

The picture names in each row rhyme. Write the picture names.

old

low

float

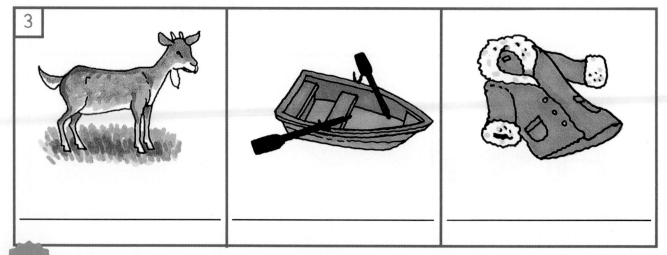

Long Vowel: / ō / o, oa, o-e, ow • Phonograms   Phonics Practice Book

Harcourt Brace School Publishers

Name _____

The **oa** in **coat**, the **o-e** in **bone**, the **ow** in **bow**, and the **o** in **comb** can all stand for the long **o** sound. Write the words where they belong in the chart. Then draw a picture for the last word in each column.

row	cold	goat	no
globe	note	grow	soap
gold	road	broke	snow

c<u>oa</u>t	b<u>o</u>n<u>e</u>	b<u>ow</u>	c<u>o</u>mb
_____	_____	_____	_____
_____	_____	_____	_____
_____	_____	_____	_____

Name _____

Circle and write the word that best completes each sentence.

1. At night I _____ to take my bath.	_____	goat	go	good
2. I like to have the water hot, not _____.	_____	cone	cot	cold
3. I take a big bar of _____.	_____	snow	soap	sap
4. I like to put a little _____ in the tub.	_____	but	boat	blown
5. It is on a long _____.	_____	rip	roll	rope
6. I like to _____ in the water.	_____	float	fold	flat
7. I _____ in the tub for a long time.	_____	soak	sold	sock
8. At last I let the water _____ down the drain.	_____	phone	fog	flow
9. Then I get out and put on my _____.	_____	robe	rob	row

Long Vowel / ō /o, oa, o-e, ow • Reading Words with Long o   Phonics Practice Book

Harcourt Brace School Publishers

Name _____

Choose the word from the box that matches each clue. Write the word to complete the puzzle.

| bone | go | home | mole | note | over |
| pole | rose | shone | smoke | stone | stove |

ACROSS
2. a small rock
4. on top of
6. where you live
8. what the sun did
10. A flame can make this.
12. A flag goes on it.

DOWN
1. You put a pot on it.
3. something for a dog to eat
5. a flower
7. to not stay
9. a thank-you _____
11. an animal

Harcourt Brace School Publishers

Circle the answer to each question. Then circle the long **o** word in the question, and write it on the line.

1. Can a car be on a (road)?	road	(Yes)	No
2. Is a baby very old?	_____	Yes	No
3. Can a ring be made from gold?	_____	Yes	No
4. Does a toad fly?	_____	Yes	No
5. Does a crow fly?	_____	Yes	No
6. Can water come from a hose?	_____	Yes	No
7. Can you fold a rock?	_____	Yes	No
8. Do you see with your nose?	_____	Yes	No
9. Can a pole have a flag on it?	_____	Yes	No
10. Is snow hot?	_____	Yes	No
11. Can a rose be red?	_____	Yes	No
12. Do you row a truck?	_____	Yes	No

Long Vowel: / ō / *o, oa, o-e, ow* • Reading Words in Context

Name _____

Do what the sentences tell you.

1. Look for the open door. Put a bow on it.

2. Find the coat. Put a hat next to it.

3. Go to the bone. Circle it.

4. Do you see the hose? Color it green.

5. Find the road. Put a toad on it.

6. Do you see the goat? Put a rope around its neck.

7. Go to the colt. Make some green grass next to him.

8. Find the smoke. Put an **X** on it.

Now circle the words that have the long **o** sound.

Harcourt Brace School Publishers

Name _____

If I could sail upon the sea,
I'd see whatever there was to see.
I'd hope to see a great big whale
Dive into the water and splash with its tail.

One day I would be inside my boat.
On the waves I would float.
I would see a rainbow fish.
Then I would have gotten my wish.

1. What would splash with its tail? _____
2. What kind of fish
   would the girl see? _____

Draw a whale and a rainbow fish to add to the picture.

Review of Long Vowels: / ā / ai, ay, a-e; ō o, oa, o-e, ow
• Reading Words in Context

Phonics Practice Book

Name _____

Look at the picture. Circle the word that completes the sentence.
Write it on the line.

1	We stay to play in the _____.	saw snow snack
2	There is an old rope across the _____.	trail train tell
3	The _____ rides in the boat!	get goat gate
4	The children like to play in the _____.	hay hog howl
5	A foal sees a _____ by the lake.	sack snail snake
6	The mole dug a _____ near the gate.	hail hill hole

Name _____

Say the name of the picture in the box. Circle the picture whose name rhymes with it.

Long Vowel: / ī / • Phonemic Awareness

Phonics Practice Book

Harcourt Brace School Publishers

Name _____

Help the child get to the . Color the pictures whose names have the vowel sound you hear in the middle of .

Name _____

The letters **i-e** often stand for the long **i** sound. Write the letters **i-e** to complete each picture name that has the long **i** sound. Then trace the whole word.

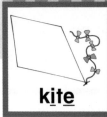

k**i**t**e**

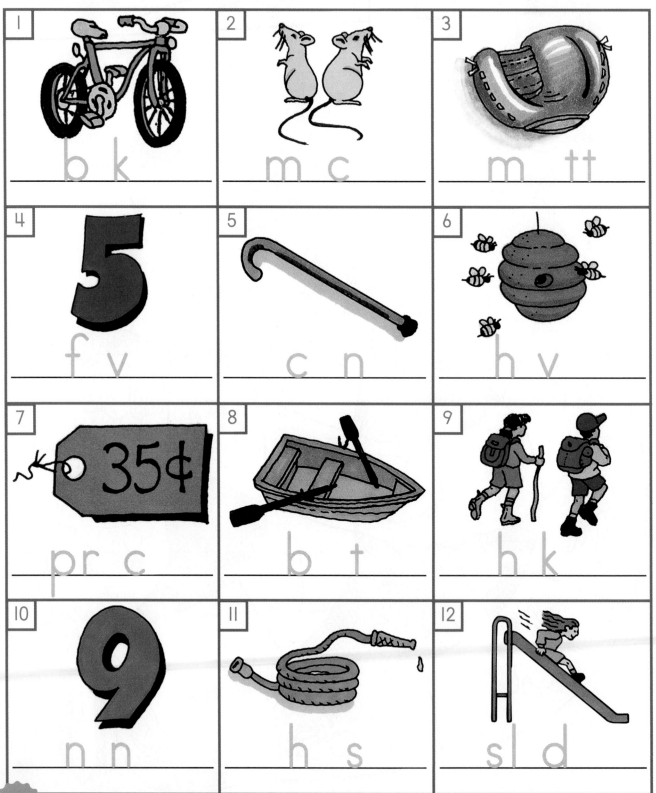

1. b___k

2. m___c

3. m___tt

4. f___v

5. c___n

6. h___v

7. pr___c

8. b___t

9. h___k

10. n___n

11. h___s

12. sl___d

Long Vowel: / ī / i-e, igh

Phonics Practice Book

Name _____

light

The letters **igh** often stand for the long **i** sound. Circle the long **i** word in each sentence.

1. Beth slept in a tent last night.
2. She could hear an owl high up in a tree.
3. The sound it made gave her a fright.
4. It sounded as if the owl wanted to fight.
5. Beth turned on her light.
6. The owl took off in flight.

Write each word you circled. Circle the letters that stand for the long **i** sound. Then draw a picture for the word.

1	2	3

4	5	6

The letter **i** can stand for the long **i** sound.
Circle the long **i** words in the sentences.

ch_i_ld

1. When Ben was a child, he played in the woods.
2. He looked for animals that lived in the wild.
3. Once he did find a mouse to look at.
4. Ben watched it stand up on its hind legs.
5. Ben still watches animals, and now he makes ones that wind up.
6. How do I know? I'm Ben!

Write each word you circled. Circle the letter that stands for the long **i** sound. Then draw a picture for the word.

1	2	3

4	5	6

Harcourt Brace School Publishers

Name _____

When **y** is at the end of a one-syllable word, it often stands for the long **i** sound. Write **y** to complete each picture name that ends with the long **i** sound. Then trace the whole word.

cr_y_

1. fr

2. fl

3. tr

4. cr

5. Wet   Not Wet
dr

6. sn

7. b

8. sk

9. sp

Name _____

Clouds

I like to look up in the sky
To see the animals flying by.
Dogs and cats and cows and pigs
All fly by and look so big!

My eyes see animals near and far.
I try to think of what they are.
Why, I ask, do animals try
To look like clouds up in the sky?

1. The animals fly by in the _____ .

2. I _____ to watch them.

3. I use _____ eyes to see the animals.

4. The animals _____ to look like clouds!

Name _____

pie

The letters **ie** can stand for the long **i** sound.
Write **ie** to complete each picture name that has the
long **i** sound. Then trace the whole word.

1. t ___

2. p ___   s

3. b ___

4. fl ___   s

5. dr ___   s

6. cr ___

7. l ___

8. tr ___

9. t ___   s

Slide and read the word. Circle and color the picture it names.

1 f i v e	
2 t i e	
3 c h i l d	
4 f l y	
5 n i g h t	

Long Vowel: / ī / i-e, igh, i, y, ie • Blending   Phonics Practice Book

The picture names in each row rhyme. Write the rhyming words.

f<u>ine</u>

_____   _____   _____

m<u>y</u>

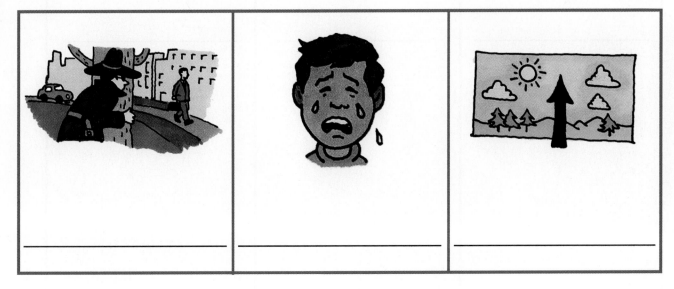

_____   _____   _____

The **i-e** in **five,** the **y** in **fry,** and the **ie** in **ties** all stand for the long **i** sound.

Write the words where they belong in the chart. Then draw a picture for the last word in each column.

dive	fly	slide
pie	tie	cry
sky	ride	dries

f<u>i</u>v<u>e</u>	fr<u>y</u>	t<u>ie</u>s
_____	_____	_____
_____	_____	_____
_____	_____	_____

Name _____

1. I came here on my _____ .   book   bike   back

2. It was fun to _____ .   raid   rid   ride

3. I brought a _____ with a   kite   kit   kind
   long tail.

4. I will _____ it.   fly   flag   flow

5. Will it go up very _____ ?   hay   hog   high

6. It flies in the _____ !   she   sky   skip

7. Later I'll play on the _____ .   slide   slid   slow

8. It is right _____ the swings.   bee   by   boy

9. I have _____ dimes.   find   fish   five

10. I'll get _____-cream!   ice   age   ink

Name _____

Circle 13 long **i** words hidden in the puzzle. Some words go across. Some words go down.

```
S H Y F L Y W O
K X Q I I P E I
Y T F G G I C C
B C I H H E H E
I R V T T Y I E
K Y E T I E L A
E Z X W I L D Z
```

Write a word from the puzzle to name each picture.

1 	2 	3 	4 
_____	_____	_____	_____

5 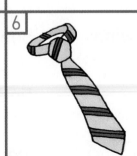	6 	7 	8 
_____	_____	_____	_____

Long Vowel: / ī / *i-e, igh, i, y, ie* • Reading Words with Long *i*   Phonics Practice Book

Name _____

Circle the answer to each question. Then circle the long **i** word in the question and write it on the line.

1. Do some people (fry) eggs? _____fry_____ (Yes) No

2. Are most mice green? _____ Yes No

3. Is night the same as day? _____ Yes No

4. Can a flag have a stripe? _____ Yes No

5. Are some animals wild? _____ Yes No

6. Do cows fly? _____ Yes No

7. Can some people dive into water? _____ Yes No

8. Can a sandwich cry? _____ Yes No

9. Might a shark walk? _____ Yes No

10. Is a dog one kind of animal? _____ Yes No

11. Is five more than ten? _____ Yes No

12. Do some people eat pies? _____ Yes No

Name _____

The sun is bright. Kay and Mike are going for a hike with their mom. They like to smell the pine trees in the woods. They like to find wild animals to look at, too. When a bird flies by, Kay and Mike always smile. Kay and Mike talk while they walk. They will be walking for a long time, but they do not mind.

Now write the long **i** word that completes each sentence.

l. Kay and Mike walk a long way on their _____.

2. They like the smell of the _____ trees.

3. Kay and Mike like to look at _____ animals.

4. Kay and Mike _____ because they are happy.

5. They do not _____ the long walk.

Long Vowel: /ī/ *i-e, igh, i, y, ie* • Reading Words in Context   Phonics Practice Book

Say the name of the picture in the first box. Circle the picture whose name rhymes with it.

1			

2			

3			

4			

5			

Dean stops to fix his  . Color the pictures whose names have the sound you hear in the middle of

The letters **ee** often stand for the long **e** sound. Write **ee** to complete each picture name that has the long **e** sound. Then trace the whole word.

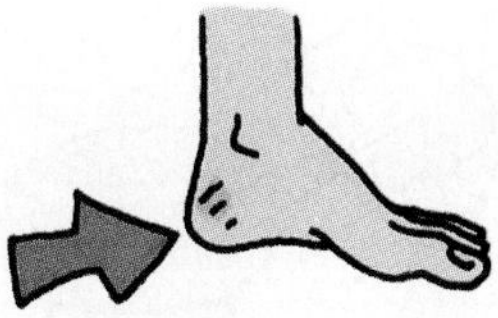

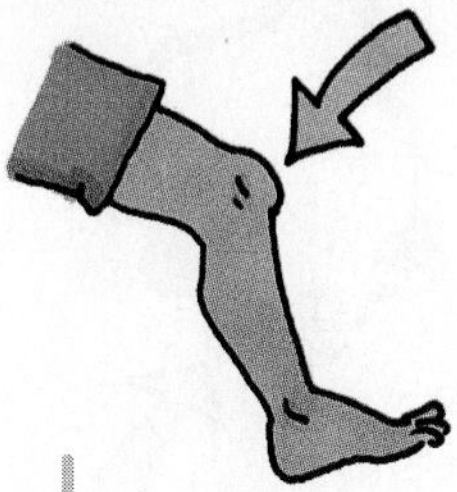

sheep

1	2	3
h____l	thr____	b____d
4	5	6
kn____	n____t	tr____
7	8	9
j____p	wh____l	p____l
10	11	12
s____p	b____	wh____l

Name _____

The letters **ea** often stand for the long **e** sound. Write **ea** to complete each picture name that has the long **e** sound. Then trace the whole word.

1   l   f ___

2   t   d ___

3   st   m ___

4   fl ___

5   s   l ___

6   b   d ___

7   dr   m ___

8   b   k ___

9   k   te ___

10   r   d ___

11   b   ll ___

12   t   m ___

f ield The letters **ie** sometimes stand for the long **e** sound. Circle the long **e** word in each sentence.

1. Look at the knight in the field.
2. His name is Willie.
3. I think this is the chief of all the knights.
4. Where is his shield?
5. Listen to the knight shriek!
6. I hope the yell is brief.

Write each word you circled. Circle the letters that stand for the long **e** sound. Then draw a picture for the word.

1	2	3
_____	_____	_____
4	**5**	**6**
_____	_____	_____

Name _____

When the letter **y** is at the end of a two-syllable word, it usually stands for the long **e** sound. Circle the long **e** word in each sentence.

baby

1. Listen to this story that I will tell.

2. It is about a family.

3. They lived in a great big city.

4. One day a funny thing took place.

5. A bunny hopped in the door.

6. Now the rabbit and the puppy are best friends.

Write each word you circled. Circle the letter that stands for the long **e** sound. Then draw a picture for the word.

1	2	3
_____	_____	_____

4	5	6
_____	_____	_____

Harcourt Brace School Publishers

Name _____

1.
Daddy is happy.
Daddy is hot.
Daddy is angry.

2.
A clown can fly in the sky.
A clown does a silly trick.
A clown sits on the funny seat.

3.
She is very hungry.
She has a lot of company.
She points to a country.

4.
I will fry some eggs.
I will play a game.
I will study for the test.

5.
My dog is all soapy.
I tell my dog a story.
The puppy sees a silly bunny.

6.
It is a cloudy morning.
It is a rainy morning.
It is a sunny morning.

Name_____

Slide and read the word. Circle and color the picture it names.

1	 s e a l			

2	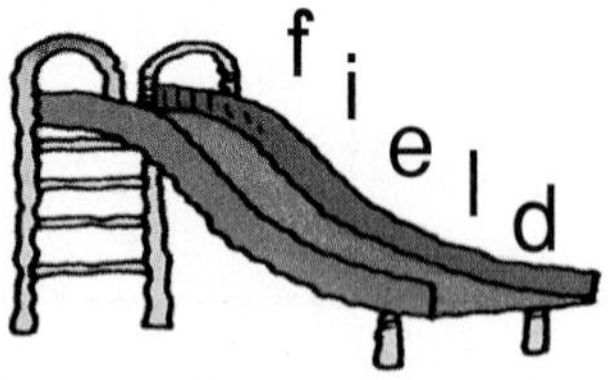 f i e l d			

3	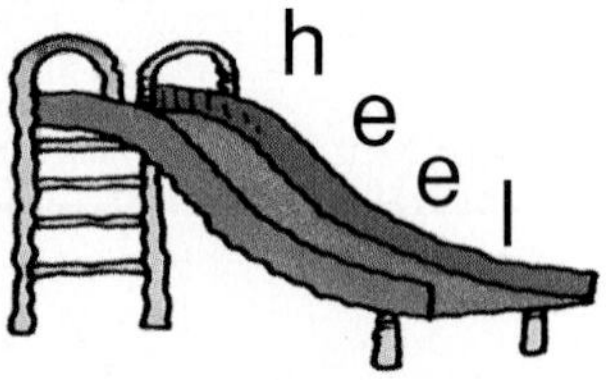 h e e l			

4	 p u p p y			

5	r e a d			

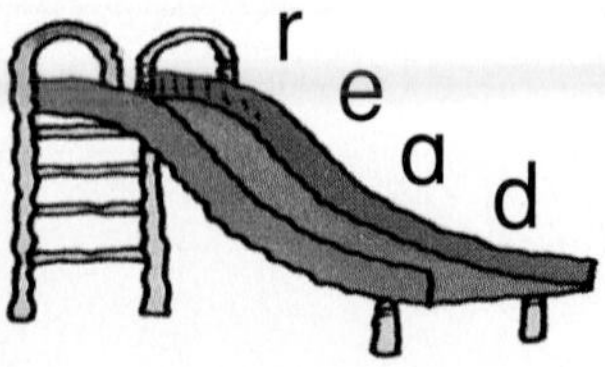

Harcourt Brace School Publishers

Long Vowel: / ē / ee, ea, ie, y • Blending

Phonics Practice Book

Name _____

1. f**eel**

2. k**eep**

3. b**ea**m

Long Vowel: / ē / *ee, ea, ie, y* • Phonograms

Harcourt Brace School Publishers

115

The **ee** in **feet,** the **ea** in **beak,** the **ie** in **yield,** and the **y** in **puppy** all stand for the long **e** sound.

Write the words where they belong in the chart. Then draw a picture for the last word you write in each column.

bee	leaf	family	sheep
field	chief	leap	hungry
bunny	beach	shield	sweep

| f<u>ee</u>t | b<u>ea</u>k | y<u>ie</u>ld | pupp<u>y</u> |

Long Vowel: / ē / *ee, ea, ie, y* • Sorting Words with Long *e*   Phonics Practice Book

Harcourt Brace School Publishers

Name _____

Circle and write the word that best completes each sentence.

1. It was a _____ day.   sunny   shy   stay

2. I went up a _____ hill.   stop   step   steep

3. I saw a _____ with cold
   water.   creek   clock   crept

4. It was very _____ .   dip   deep   deal

5. I sat under a _____ .   try   tray   tree

6. I ate a _____ .   peach   porch   penny

7. The tree was by a _____ .   fed   field   fold

8. The grass was _____ .   green   groan   grin

9. I could feel the sun's _____ . hit   hay   heat

10. It made me _____ .   sleepy   sly   sky

Name _____

Choose the word that matches each clue. Write the words to complete the puzzle.

deep   feed   feet   field   keep   leak   heel
pretty   read   see   sleep   speedy   weed   wheels

ACROSS

1. A bike has two.
3. It is part of a foot.
4. It means "to not give away."
7. Crops grow here.
9. You do this with your eyes.
10. It means "to give food to."
11. It means "fast."

DOWN

1. It is a plant.
2. This is a drip.
5. It looks nice. It is _____.
6. You do this with a book.
7. They are on your legs.
8. The sea is very _____.
9. You do this at night.

Long Vowel: / ē / *ee, ea, ie, y* • Reading Words with Long *e*   Phonics Practice Book

Harcourt Brace School Publishers

Circle the long **e** word in each question, and write it on the line. Then circle the answer to each question.

1. Do you put a hat on
   your (feet)?   _____feet_____   Yes   (No)

2. Is a cherry blue?   _____   Yes   No

3. Does a hen have a beak?   _____   Yes   No

4. Does a leaf grow on a pig?   _____   Yes   No

5. Does grass grow in a field?   _____   Yes   No

6. Does a sheet go on a bed?   _____   Yes   No

7. Can you ride in a jeep?   _____   Yes   No

8. Can a seal fly?   _____   Yes   No

9. Can a dog have fleas?   _____   Yes   No

10. Is a shriek a loud noise?   _____   Yes   No

Name _____

1. Do you see a peach? Color it green.

2. Find the hat for the chief. Color it red.

3. Add some meat for the man to eat.

4. Can you find a tea bag? Circle it.

5. Find the pot on the stove. Make steam over it.

6. Where will the lady sit? Make a seat for her.

7. Who will peel the peach? Put a bowl on her knee.

8. Who will sweep the rug? Circle his feet.

Now circle the words that have the long **e** sound.

Find the name of each picture. Write the word on the line.

kite	beak	dry	leaf
nine	light	tree	child
baby	tie	bee	dream

1

_____

2

_____

3

_____

4

_____

5

_____

6

_____

7

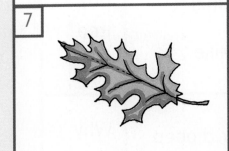

_____

8

_____

9

_____

10

Wet   Not Wet

_____

11

_____

12

_____

Name _____

Look at the picture. Circle and write the word that completes the sentence.

1		Why is Sally so _____ today?	hay happy hurry
2		The sun is high and _____ in the sky.	bright beat boat
3		"Let's play _____ -and- seek," says Mike. "Don't peek!"	hide heed had
4		"She won't see me behind this _____ ," thinks Mike.	tray tree try
5		"_____ do I hear a peep and a cheep?" asks Mike.	Why We Way
6		"Sally didn't _____ me, but the baby jays did!"	feed fade find

Review of Long Vowels: / ī / i-e, igh, i, y, ie; / ē / ee, ea, ie, y

Phonics Practice Book

Name _____

mule

The letters **u-e** can stand for the vowel sound you hear in **mule.** Circle the word with this vowel sound in each sentence.

1. One day I saw three mules in the field.
2. They were next to a huge rock.
3. "What cute animals," I said to my dad.
4. "I think they would like these ice cubes."
5. "What would they use them for?" asked my dad.
6. "I don't know," I said. "I'm not a mule!"

Write each word you circled. Then draw a picture for the word.

1	2	3

4	5	6

Name _____

 1	The baby is very cute. The baby has a big cut. The cute baby is on a mule.
 2	A cub is in the cup. A mule wants some water. A cube will make the water cold.
3	A huge animal is next to the boat. We hug the big animal. Mom hugs me on the boat.
 4	The girl is on a mouse. The girl rides the mule. The mule and the girl sit down.
 5	I have a huge tray. I can play in this huge yard. I use this to play today.

Long Vowel: / yōō / u-e • Reading Words in Context

Phonics Practice Book

Name _____

The Animal Parade

Follow these directions
    and do your best.
Put an eagle in its nest.

Find the pony running by.
Make it yellow. Be sure to try!

Where is the lion? It is huge!
Color its mane. What color
will you use?

A goat and a crow are marching by.
Color green the one that can fly!

A tiger is creeping on the trail.
Put black and yellow stripes on its tail.

Now you are done with the animal parade.
Do you like what you have made?

Harcourt Brace School Publishers

Name _____

Look at the picture. Circle and write the word that completes each sentence.

1	He will dry his mane after a day in the _____ .	ran rain run
2	Can a goat tell _____ if the bells do not chime?	time tame team
3	Will a flea be a _____ for a year or a week?	chain chief chase
4	Does a _____ sail in the deep blue sea?	whale while why
5	Blow a _____ bubble and watch it fly high.	hug heap huge
6	Oak trees _____ to reach the sky, and so do I.	tray try three

Harcourt Brace School Publishers

Cumulative Review: Long Vowels

Phonics Practice Book

Name _____

Fill in the circle next to the name of each picture.

1
- ○ sheep
- ○ ship
- ○ shape

2
- ○ sill
- ○ sole
- ○ sail

3
- ○ light
- ○ late
- ○ let

4
- ○ bat
- ○ boat
- ○ bite

5
- ○ try
- ○ tray
- ○ tree

6
- ○ fold
- ○ fade
- ○ field

7
- ○ can
- ○ cone
- ○ cane

8
- ○ mile
- ○ mule
- ○ mail

9
- ○ soapy
- ○ say
- ○ spy

10
- ○ seal
- ○ sole
- ○ sell

11
- ○ body
- ○ bow
- ○ bay

12
- ○ rock
- ○ rack
- ○ rake

13
- ○ cube
- ○ cab
- ○ cub

14
- ○ cold
- ○ chilled
- ○ child

15
- ○ pea
- ○ pie
- ○ pay

Name _____

Fill in the circle next to the sentence that tells about the picture.

1

○ I will take a boat.

○ I will take a bite.

○ I will take a bat.

2

○ The knight has a shield.

○ I showed you a knot.

○ There is a knot in the rope.

3

○ Look up at the kite.

○ The kite is in the tree.

○ A cloud is in the sky.

4

○ It is near a cat.

○ It is a happy colt.

○ It is very cute.

5

○ It will go on the pole.

○ It will go onto the peel.

○ It will go into a pail.

6

○ Let's go up a tree.

○ Let's go in a truck.

○ Let's go on a train.

Test: Long Vowels

Phonics Practice Book

Name _____

Circle and write the word that answers each riddle.

1. They are on your legs. _____ feet   fat   fight

2. It keeps things together. _____ tap   tip   tape

3. You can sleep in it. _____ bed   bead   bad

4. You can drink from it. _____ cap   cup   cape

5. It means "very, very big." _____ huge   hug   hang

6. You can fly in it. _____ plan   play   plane

7. You can carry water in it. _____ pill   pail   pole

8. A puppy may be one. _____ pet   pot   pit

9. You can play it on a friend. _____ trick   truck   track

10. It may live in a field. _____ gate   got   goat

Harcourt Brace School Publishers

Name _____

Read each word. Add a vowel to write a word with a long vowel sound. Draw a picture for each new word.

1. got	_____	
2. cub	_____	
3. cot	_____	
4. ran	_____	
5. tap	_____	
6. pin	_____	
7. set	_____	
8. bed	_____	

Harcourt Brace School Publishers

Cumulative Review: Short and Long Vowels

Phonics Practice Book

Name _____

Fill in the circle next to the name of each picture.

 CHECK-UP

1
- ○ goat
- ○ get
- ○ gate

2
- ○ cat
- ○ cot
- ○ coat

3
- ○ toad
- ○ tide
- ○ tail

4
- ○ ten
- ○ tan
- ○ teen

5
- ○ ran
- ○ run
- ○ rain

6
- ○ bay
- ○ baby
- ○ by

7
- ○ mile
- ○ mail
- ○ mule

8
- ○ pine
- ○ pin
- ○ pan

9
- ○ bread
- ○ braid
- ○ bride

10
- ○ keep
- ○ kite
- ○ kit

11
- ○ wheel
- ○ well
- ○ whale

12
- ○ tab
- ○ tube
- ○ tub

Phonics Practice Book

Test: Short and Long Vowels

131

CHECK-UP

Fill in the circle next to the sentence that tells about the picture.

1.
○ The mole is on the bat.
○ The mole is in the boat.
○ The mole bit the bait.

2.
○ Eva might get a red mitten.
○ Eva will sit on a mat.
○ Eva will use her mitt.

3.
Pet Store
○ This little cat is a cute kitty.
○ The coat is on the kitty's tail.
○ The cat sits on a kite.

4.
○ The chief rides in the truck.
○ The chief did a funny trick.
○ The chief has climbed a tree.

5.
○ Jay and Pat ride in a funny boat.
○ Jay and Pat ride on a sunny day.
○ Jay and Pat row as fast as they can.

6.
○ The sheep stands in a field.
○ The ship is far away.
○ The field is a good place to shop.

Test: Short and Long Vowels

Name _____

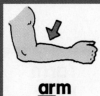
arm

The letters **ar** often stand for the vowel sound you hear in **arm**. Write **ar** to complete each picture name that has the same vowel sound as **arm.** Then trace the whole word.

1	2	3
st___	b___n	b___t
4	**5**	**6**
c___t	c___p	sh___k
7	**8**	**9**
f___n	y___n	j___
10	**11**	**12**
c___d	sc___f	p___n

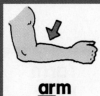

Name _____

Write the word that completes each sentence.

yard	dark	large	started	farm
March	stars	far	barn	bark

1. It is very _____ at night.

2. I like to look at the sky to see the _____ .

3. They are very _____ away.

4. Sometimes when I'm outside, I hear a dog

   _____ .

5. The dog lives on the _____ next to ours.

6. The dog is very _____ .

7. It sleeps in the hay inside a _____ .

8. Once I slept in a tent in our _____ .

9. It _____ to snow!

10. I'll never sleep outside in _____ again!

R-Controlled Vowel: /är/ *ar* • Reading Words with *ar*   Phonics Practice Book

Harcourt Brace School Publishers

Name _____

The letters **er** and **ur** often stand for the vowel sound you hear in **fern** and **turtle**. Write the word that completes each sentence.

f<u>er</u>n

t<u>ur</u>tle

curb	nurse	perch	germs	her
turns	surprised	fern	hurt	purse

1. My mom goes to _____ job every morning.

2. She puts everything she needs in her _____.

3. Then she walks out the door and _____ left.

4. She gets on the bus at the _____.

5. Mom takes care of children who are _____.

6. She helps children get rid of bad _____.

7. Every day I _____ on the steps and wait for

   Mom to come home.

8. Last Thursday, I gave her a pretty _____.

9. She was very _____.

10. What is my mom? She is a _____.

Name _____

1. Do you see the clerk? Make her dress red.
2. Find an animal with fur. Make a ring around it.
3. Can you find a fern? Make the fern green.
4. Where is the nurse? Make her purse blue.
5. Do you see a turkey? Put a blue **O** on it.
6. Find the turtle. Make the turtle purple.
7. Find the name of a day. Make a red **X** on it.
8. Do you see something that will turn? Color it yellow.

The letters **ir** often stand for the vowel sound you hear in **bird**. Write **ir** to complete each word that has the same vowel sound as **bird**. Then trace the whole word.

b**ir**d

1. g __ l	2. sk __ t	3. w __ g
4. cl __ p	5. sh __ t	6. st __
7. f __ st	8. th __ d	9. s __ x
10. d __ t	11. tw __ ns	12. b __ thday

Name _____

Circle the sentence that tells about the picture.

---

1 	First we will put in a stick. First we will give it a stir. First we will look at a star.
2	The birds are on a perch. One bird has a shirt. Here comes the third bird.
3 	There are five trees. There are three birds in the trees. There are some fir trees.
4 	She has on a skirt and a shirt. She skips in a shirt and pants. She got dirt on her scarf.
5 	The boy and the goat get some dirt. The boy and the girl twirl in the dirt. The boy and the girl twirl a goat.
6 	A girl walks her dog. A girl twirls with her dog. A girl sees a dog in a skirt.

R-controlled Vowel: / ûr / *ir* • Reading Words in Context

Name _____

p<u>ear</u>l

The letters **ear** sometimes stand for the vowel sound you hear in **pearl.** Write the word that names each picture.

Earth	heard	early	pearls	learn	search

1. _____

2. _____

3. _____

4. _____

5. _____

6. _____

Write the word from above that best completes each sentence about the pictures.

1. Elephant will _____ at school.

2. Elephant will _____ for Lion.

3. Elephant likes the _____.

4. Elephant gets up _____.

5. Elephant looks down to see _____.

6. Elephant _____ her mom.

REVIEW

Choose the word that matches each clue. Then write the words to complete the puzzle.

barn	burn	clerk	far	third	learn
park	search	shirt	stirs	turtle	whirl

ACROSS
1. someone who works in a shop
4. something you put on
6. to look for
7. a house for animals
8. first, second, ____
9. not close
10. a place with trees and grass

DOWN
2. to find out something
3. to turn very fast
5. a very slow animal
6. mixes
7. what hot fires do

Review of *R*-controlled Vowels: / är / *ar*; / ûr / *er, ur, ir, ear*

Phonics Practice Book

Harcourt Brace School Publishers

Name _____

1. What rhymes with **twirl** and is not a boy?

   _____

2. What rhymes with **card** and means "not easy"?

   _____

3. What rhymes with **star** and is something you can ride in?

   _____

4. What rhymes with **shirt** and is what you put plants in?

   _____

5. What rhymes with **burn** and tells what you do when you

   go another way?

   _____

6. What rhymes with **purse** and names someone who can

   help you?

   _____

7. What rhymes with **fir** and tells what you might call a man?

   _____

Name _____

Write the word that completes each sentence.

dirt	learn	bark	birds	third
march	herd	fur	turn	far

1. I am in the _____ grade.

2. Today my class will _____ about cats.

3. I will have a _____ to tell about my cat.

4. My cat has black _____ .

5. She likes to _____ down the street with other cats.

6. They look like a _____ of cats!

7. Once my cat chased some _____ .

8. But they did fly _____ away.

9. My cat likes to play in the _____ .

10. She does not like to hear dogs _____ .

Harcourt Brace School Publishers

Review of *R*-controlled Vowels: / är / *ar;* / ûr / *er, ur, ir, ear*   Phonics Practice Book

Help the  find its home. Color each picture whose name has the sound you hear at the beginning of [owl] and in the middle of [cloud].

Name _____

The letters **ow** or **ou** can stand for the vowel sound you hear in **owl** and **house**. Write the word that names each picture.

owl

house

hound   cloud   crown   cow   mouse   clown

1. _____

2. _____

3. _____

4. _____

5. _____

6. _____

Write each picture name from above in the correct column.

owl

_____

_____

_____

house

_____

_____

_____

Vowel Diphthong: / ou / *ow, ou* • Sorting Words with *ow, ou*

Phonics Practice Book

Name _____

howl	crowd	sound	town	clouds
ground	clowns	growl	round	crown

1. One day the king was in _____.

2. A very big _____ came to see him.

3. Everybody was on the _____ in the grass.

4. Big _____ were in the sky.

5. The king had a big _____ on his head.

6. It was _____.

7. It had pictures of happy, dancing _____ on it.

8. My dog started to _____.

9. The king must have liked the _____ because he started to bark.

10. That made the rest of us laugh and _____.

Name ─────────────────────────

Read the poem. Then complete the sentences.

 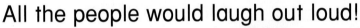 **The Clown**

I want to be a funny clown
Who likes to jump up and down.
I'd have a nose that is red and
  round.
I'd stand on my hands to walk on
  the ground.

I'd paint on a smile, never a frown.
And every time I was in town,
I'd do my tricks in front of a crowd.
All the people would laugh out loud!

1. This _____ would be funny.

2. The red nose would be _____.

3. The mouth would not have a _____.

4. People in the _____ would laugh out loud.

Vowel Diphthong: / ou / *ow, ou* • Reading Words in Context   Phonics Practice Book

Name _____

 horn   core   four

Write the word that names each picture.

snore   pour   fourth   corn   store
shore   horse   court   fork

1	2	3
_____	_____	_____

4	5	6
_____	_____	_____

7	8	9
_____	_____	_____

Name _____

door

oar

The letters **oor** and **oar** usually stand for the vowel sound you hear in **door** and **oar.**
Write the word that answers each riddle.

roar	board	floor	oar
poor	soar	door	boar

1. You put a rug on me. _____

2. I am part of a game. _____

3. I am a loud animal sound. _____

4. You can open me. _____

5. You row a boat with me. _____

6. I mean "to fly." _____

7. I am a wild animal. _____

8. I mean "not rich." _____

148

Write the word that answers each riddle.

1. I am something to eat that rhymes with *horn.*

   What am I? _____

2. I am a small animal, and I rhyme with *house.*

   What am I? _____

3. I come after three and rhyme with *pour.*

   What am I? _____

4. I make you laugh and rhyme with *down.*

   What am I? _____

5. I am something you open and shut. I rhyme with *floor.*

   What am I? _____

6. I am a big animal, and I rhyme with *how.*

   What am I? _____

7. I tell where you shop and rhyme with *core.*

   What am I? _____

8. I am an animal sound that rhymes with *oar.*

   What am I? _____

Name _____

1. Find the horse. Color it brown.
2. Look for the cow. Give it another horn.
3. What will the boar eat? Circle the core.
4. Who might pounce on the mouse? Make an **X** on it.
5. What sound will the owl make? Make a cloud by the owl and write WHO in it.
6. Count four pigs. Color them red.
7. Find the house. Make a door for it.
8. Who tore her shirt on the thorn? Color her shorts blue.

Harcourt Brace School Publishers

boy

point

The letters **oi** and **oy** usually stand for the vowel sound you hear in **point** and **boy**. Read the story. Then draw a picture to show what happens in the story. Use words from the story to label things in your picture.

Hi, I'm Joy.

My name is Joy. I am a girl dog, not a boy dog. Today I dug a hole in the garden soil. First I found my lost toy. Then I found some coins. Today was a day I did enjoy!

Now circle all the words that have the vowel sound you hear in **point** and **boy**.

Name _____

Write the word from the box that best completes the sentence.

| points | soil | cowboys | join |
| enjoy | noise | boiled | coiled |

1. We _____ going on long rides on horses.

2. We make believe we are cowgirls and _____ .

3. Once we heard a snake's loud _____ .

4. We saw a snake in the dirt, or _____ .

5. The snake was _____ , so we rode away.

6. Another time, we rode to a place where two streams

_____ , or come together.

7. We camped near a big rock with five _____ on it.

8. Then we _____ water over the hot campfire.

Vowel Diphthong: / oi / *oi, oy* • Reading Words with *oi, oy*   Phonics Practice Book

Name _____

Circle the sentence that tells about the picture.

1	The boy spills a glass of water. The boy puts it away so it will not spoil. The boy puts it in some soil.
2	Joy gets a toy for her birthday. Joy points to the tent. Joy finds a coin on her birthday.
3	She boils some soup in a pot. She puts water in a pot to boil. She fills the pot with soil.
4	Troy hears an owl. Troy puts oil on the sail. Troy has an oyster shell.
5	The toy drum is on the table. The drum makes a loud noise. The noise comes from the dogs.
6	The dime has three points on it. The toy paints are mine. It points to the dime.

Name _____

Circle and write the word that answers the riddle.

1. You sometimes play with me. _____ boil   toy   enjoy

2. I can be a dime or a quarter. _____ coil   foil   coin

3. I am at the end of a pencil. _____ point   cowboy oil

4. I mean "happy." _____ boys   joyful join

5. You can plant in me. _____ snail   soy   soil

6. I am what a pig says. _____ oink   oil   joy

7. I am what very hot water does. _____ boils   bays   boys

8. I am a very loud sound. _____ moist   noise   broil

9. I mean "not good anymore." _____ spoiled loyal   annoyed

Vowel Diphthong: / oi / oi, oy • Reading Words with oi, oy   Phonics Practice Book

Name _____

The letters **oo** sometimes stand for the vowel sound you hear in **foot.** Write the letters **oo** to complete each picture name that has the vowel sound you hear in **foot.** Then trace the whole word.

f<u>oo</u>t

1	h___k	2	br___k	3	b___ne
4	w___l	5	p___l	6	c___k
7	l___ck	8	b___k	9	h___d
10	w___d	11	p___t	12	f___t

Vowel Variant: / o͝o / *oo*

Name _____

Do what the sentences tell you.

1. Find two children looking at a book. Color the book green.
2. Do you see a girl with a sheep? Make her stick look like a hook.
3. Who took a plum? Color the plum blue.
4. Which girl's bowl fell? Draw a circle around her.
5. One little pig makes his house of wood. Color the wood brown.
6. Who has a cape with a hood? Color the cape and hood red.
7. Who cooks? Color her dress purple.

Name _____

Circle the letters that complete the word in each sentence. Then write the word on the line.

1. I always enj____ going
   to the farm.   _____   ou   ow   oy

2. I like to feel the sheep's
   soft w____l.   _____   oo   ow   oi

3. When I hear the pigs
   ____nk, I laugh.   _____   ow   oi   oo

4. The cows make
   n____se when they moo.   _____   oi   ou   oo

5. I wish that I c____ld
   ride one of the horses.   _____   oi   oy   ou

6. Grandpa let me plant my
   own beans in the s____l.   _____   ou   oi   oo

7. Today we will use
   w____d to start a fire.   _____   oo   oa   oi

8. Then we will b____l
   some water.   _____   ow   ou   oi

9. We will c____k and eat my
   beans. Yum!   _____   oo   oy   ow

Harcourt Brace School Publishers

Review of Vowel Diphthong: / oi / *oi, oy*;
Vowel Variant: / o͝o / *oo, ou*

Name _____

1. I am the part of a coat that rhymes with *wood*. What am I?   _____

2. I tell what very hot water will do. I rhyme with *foil*. What am I?   _____

3. I am fun to play with, and I rhyme with *boy*. What am I?   _____

4. I mean "not bad." I rhyme with *stood*. What am I?   _____

5. I mean "to see." I rhyme with *book*. What am I?   _____

6. I am not a girl, and I rhyme with *Roy*. What am I?   _____

7. I can be a dime. I rhyme with *join*. What am I?   _____

8. I am like a small river and rhyme with *cook*. What am I?   _____

Harcourt Brace School Publishers

Name _____

Circle the letters that complete the word in each sentence. Then write the word on the line.

1. I live in this brown
h____se.

_____   ou   or   oy

2. Open the d____ and
come inside.

_____   oy   ear   oor

3. Do you like my painting
of the cl____n?

_____   ow   oar   oi

4. W____ld you like to
see my room?

_____   ore   ou   oy

5. I have another l____ge
painting in it.

_____   ar   ur   ow

6. The painting shows a
h____d of cows.

_____   er   ar   ou

7. It also shows birds s____ing
in the sky.

_____   ur   ar   oar

8. Come in here and we
can c____k something.

_____   oy   ow   oo

9. We will wait for the
water to b____l.

_____   er   oi   ow

10. Then you can help me
st____.

_____   ar   oi   ir

Cumulative Review: / är / ar; / ûr / er, ur, ir, ear; / ôr / or,
ore, our, oor, oar; / ou / ow, ou; / oi / oi, oy; / o͞o / oo, ou

159

Name _____

Circle and write the word that best completes each sentence.

1. I went outside one
   ____ night.   _____   dirt   dock   dark

2. I could hear a
   ____ singing.   _____   bird   boil   board

3. My dog ____ me
   outside.   _____   joy   jar   joined

4. I patted it and felt
   its soft ____.   _____   far   for   fur

5. We walked ____
   the hill.   _____   down   door   den

6. But we did not go
   into the ____.   _____   words   wails   woods

7. I ____ not go in
   there at night.   _____   shark   short   should

8. I could trip and
   hurt my ____.   _____   four   fork   foot

9. All at once, it
   started to ____.   _____   pour   perk   park

10. I did not want to stay
    outside any ____.   _____   more   mole   mark

Cumulative Review: / är / ar; / ûr / er, ur, ir, ear; / ôr / or, ore,
our, oor, oar; / ou / ow, ou; / oi / oi, oy; / o͞o / oo, ou

Phonics Practice Book

Harcourt Brace School Publishers

Name _____

deer

tear

The letters **eer** and **ear** sometimes stand for the vowel sound you hear in **deer** and **tear**. Write the word that answers each riddle.

peer	fear	near	ears
cheer	hear	year	steer

1. You have two of me on your head. _____

2. I am 12 months long. _____

3. If you are afraid, you are full of me. _____

4. I am what you do when you listen. _____

5. I am what you do when you want your team to win. _____

6. I mean "not far." _____

7. I am what you do to make a bike go where you want it to. _____

8. I mean "to look at." _____

Harcourt Brace School Publishers

chair

pear

The letters **air** and **ear** sometimes stand for the vowel sound you hear in **chair** and **pear.** Read each sentence and circle the word that has the vowel sound you hear in **chair** and **pear.**

1. A bear named Len got up one morning.

2. He took a big breath of fresh air.

3. He got dressed and walked down the stairs.

4. Len sat down in the rocking chair.

5. His mother brushed his thick brown hair.

6. Then Len ate a great big pear!

Write each word you circled. Then draw a picture for it.

1	2	3
_____	_____	_____

4	5	6
_____	_____	_____

R-Controlled Vowel: / âr / *air, ear*

Phonics Practice Book

Harcourt Brace School Publishers

Name _____

Write the word that answers each riddle.

chair	pair	hair	air	fair
share	stairs	square	mare	scare

1	If you have two matching socks, you have this. _____	2	I grow on your head. _____
3	I am what you breathe. _____	4	I mean "to make someone afraid." _____
5	I am a place with rides to go on and prizes to win. _____	6	I mean "to take turns." _____
7	I am a shape. _____	8	I am something you go up and down. _____
9	I am a horse. _____	10	I am something to sit on. _____

Name _____

Circle the letters that stand for the vowel sound in each picture name. Then write the picture name on the line.

1.
air
er
ear

2.
air
ear
ar

3.
air
ir
ore

4.
ear
are
ir

5.
are
eer
ar

6.
eer
ore
air

7.
are
or
ear

8.
ir
ear
ore

9.
eer
oor
are

Harcourt Brace School Publishers

Circle the sentence that tells about the picture.

1

The deer are in the field.

The deer are near the door.

The deer are at the fair.

2

Clare wears a coat.

Clare tears a chair.

Clare eats a pear.

3

The hare stands on its ears.

The hare has one ear up.

The hare sees a bear's eyes.

4

The bear sits on the stairs.

The bear steers the car.

The bear is at the steering wheel.

5

Blair sleeps in the chair.

Blair is in the square.

Blair gets up and cheers.

6

The colt is near the mat.

The colt is near a bear.

The colt is near the mare.

Name _____

 glue    flute   jewel

Read the story. Then use words from the story to complete the sentences.

Ana's Song

Ana likes to play her flute. She can play pretty tunes on it. She wrote new words to go with one of the tunes. The words tell about birds that flew away. The birds went up in the blue sky. Ana drew a picture to go with her song.

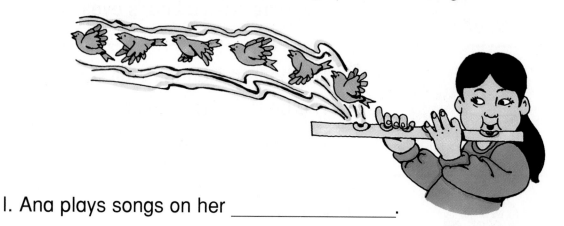

1. Ana plays songs on her _____.

2. The _____ she plays are pretty.

3. She _____ a picture for one song.

4. The picture showed a sky that was _____.

5. Birds _____ in the sky.

6. What _____ words would you write for a song?

Vowel Variant: / $\overline{oo}$ / *ue, u-e, ew* • Reading Words in Context   Phonics Practice Book

Harcourt Brace School Publishers

Name _____

Write the word that best completes each sentence.

stew	chewed	clue	flew
blue	June	cute	threw

1. I got my dog, Woof, last _____.

2. He is very _____, but he always gets into trouble.

3. Once he found my _____ socks.

4. He _____ them until they were full of holes.

5. Another time I _____ my ball to him.

6. He _____ after it and got it.

7. I don't have a _____ where he hid it!

8. Then there was that _____ that my mother cooked. It's a good thing that we love Woof!

Vowel Variant: / oo / ue, u-e, ew • Reading Words

Circle the sentence that tells about the picture.

1		Pig plays a tune on the flute. Pig gives two flutes to Frog. Pig flew to a new place.
2		Cat drew a picture of some stew. Cat did chew what he drew. Cat drew a new plant.
3		Frog blew out the light. Frog looks for a new clue. Frog uses some new glue.
4		Cat threw it to Pig. Cat knew how to kick. Cat and Pig glue it on.
5		Dog chews on the new flute. Dog chews the tube. Dog chews on the new bone.
6		Dog blew into the flute. Dog and Frog flew away. Dog flew over Frog.

Vowel Variant: / $\overline{oo}$ / ue, u-e, ew • Reading Words in Context

Phonics Practice Book

Harcourt Brace School Publishers

Name _____

Circle the answer to each question. Then circle and write the word that has the vowel sound you hear in *glue*.

1. Can people chew gum? _____ Yes No

2. Does *old* mean "new"? _____ Yes No

3. Can a queen rule? _____ Yes No

4. Is a red rose blue? _____ Yes No

5. Can something be in a tube? _____ Yes No

6. Can some people sing a tune? _____ Yes No

7. Is a lie true? _____ Yes No

8. Can people eat stew? _____ Yes No

9. Can some people play a flute? _____ Yes No

10. Does the crew help on a plane? _____ Yes No

11. Is a clue an animal? _____ Yes No

12. Can a puppy be cute? _____ Yes No

Name _____

The letters **oo** can stand for the vowel sound you hear in **zoo**.
Write the word that answers each riddle.

ZOO

1. I keep your feet dry and rhyme
with *roots*. What am I?

_____

2. I rhyme with *zoo*. I am what a
cow says. What am I?

_____

3. I rhyme with *boom*. I am part
of a house. What am?

_____

4. I am something to eat. I rhyme
with *group*. What am I?

_____

5. I am in your mouth. I rhyme
with *booth*. What am I?

_____

6. You can see me in the sky.
I rhyme with *spoon*. What am I?

_____

7. I am something to eat that rhymes
with *mood*. What am I?

_____

8. I mean "not old." I rhyme with *grew*.
What am I?

_____

Vowel Variant: / $\overline{oo}$ / oo • Writing Words

Phonics Practice Book

Name _____

Look at each picture. Write the word that makes each sentence tell about the picture.

threw   soup   zooms   boots   stool

1	This girl wears _____
2	Julio _____ to the moon.
3	Lew is on the _____
4	Cara is eating some _____
5	Eva _____ the ball.

Name _____

The letters **ou** and **ui** can stand for the vowel sound you hear in **you** and **suit.**

Write the word that completes each sentence.

y<u>ou</u>   s<u>ui</u>t

youth	juice	soup	group
you	fruit	suit	bruise

1. Another word for *child* is _____ .

2. A word that rhymes with *do* is _____ .

3. Something good to drink is _____ .

4. Something hot and good to eat on a cold day
   is _____ .

5. If three children work together, they are in the
   same _____ .

6. If you fall, you can get a _____ .

7. Pants and a jacket that go together are
   a _____ .

8. An apple is one kind of _____ .

Harcourt Brace School Publishers

Look at each picture. Then write the answer to each question.

1		Is this a clue or clay?	_____
2		Do people play a fleet or a flute?	_____
3		Are these boats or boots?	_____
4		Does she eat stew or stoop?	_____
5		Are they in a grape or a group?	_____
6		Is an apple a fruit or a foot?	_____
7		Do you sit on a stool or a steel?	_____
8		Would someone wear a seat or a suit?	_____
9		Is a dune or a done made of sand?	_____

REVIEW Do what the sentences tell you.

1. Find the juice. Put a glass under it.
2. Do you see the soup bowl? Color it green
3. Can you find the stool? Add two legs to it.
4. Find a plate, fork, and knife. Put a spoon next to the knife.
5. It is noon. Draw hands that point to 12 on the clock.
6. Do you see some fruit? Color it purple.
7. Can you find a pot of stew on the stove? Draw some steam over it.
8. Find the name of the month. Circle it.

Harcourt Brace School Publishers

Name _____

afloat

Choose the word that matches each clue. Write the word to complete the puzzle.

| away | across | ago | ashore | adult |
| asleep | arise | afraid | around | apart |

Across

2. in the past
3. on the other side
5. scared
6. not together
7. get up

Down

1. in a circle
2. not awake
4. not here
5. on the land, or on the shore
6. a grown-up

table

flow<u>er</u>

The letters **le** and **er** can stand for the end sounds you hear in **table** and **flower.** Write each word under its picture.

hammer	bottle	batter
juggle	zipper	candle
apple	skater	turtle

1

2

3

4

5

6

7

8

9

Schwa: / əl / *le*, / ər / *er*

Phonics Practice Book

Harcourt Brace School Publishers

Name _____

dawn

The letters **aw** often stand for the vowel sound you hear in **dawn.** Write the letters **aw** to complete each picture name that has the same vowel sound as **dawn.** Then trace the whole word.

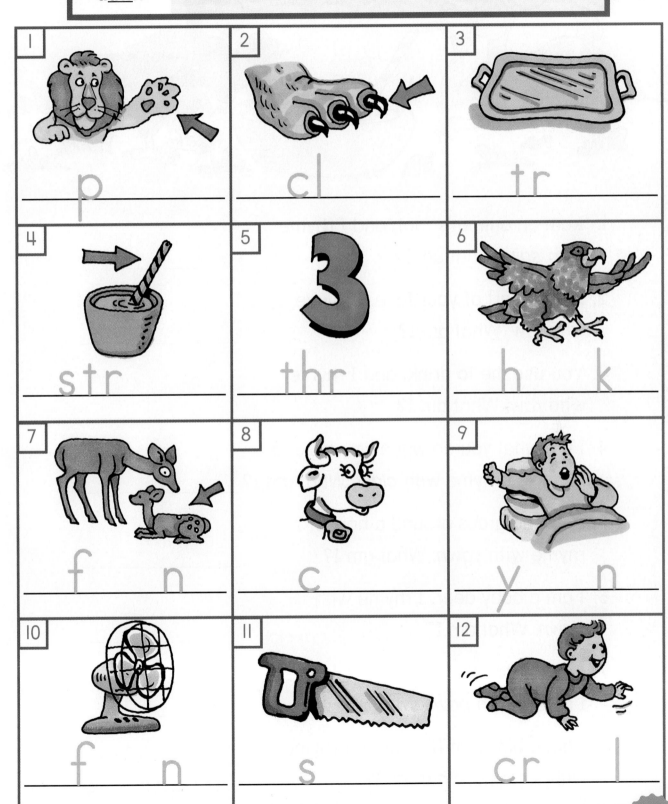

1. p ____

2. cl ____

3. tr ____

4. str ____

5. thr ____

6. h ____ k

7. f ____ n

8. c ____

9. y ____ n

10. f ____ n

11. s ____

12. cr ____ l

Name _____

1. I am an animal's foot, and I rhyme
   with *saw*. What am I?

   _____

2. I am a part of your face. I rhyme
   with *law*. What am I?

   _____

3. You use me to drink, and I rhyme
   with *raw*. What am I?

   _____

4. I am what you do when you make a
   picture. I rhyme with *claw*. What am I? _____

5. I am the grass around a house. I
   rhyme with *yawn*. What am I?

   _____

6. I am a baby deer. I rhyme with
   dawn. What am I?

   _____

7. I mean "to go on hands and knees."
   I rhyme with *bawl*. What am I?

   _____

8. I am a bird that flies high. I rhyme
   with *squawk*. What am I?

   _____

Vowel Variant: / ô / *aw* • Reading Words in Context　　　　Phonics Practice Book

Name _____

h<u>au</u>l **c<u>augh</u>t** **b<u>ough</u>t**

Write the word that completes each sentence.

because	caught	daughter	bought
brought	taught	ought	thought

1. Grandma _____ it would be fun to go fishing.

2. "I _____ to take Jenny along," said Grandma.

3. Jenny was Grandma's friend's _____.

4. So Grandma _____ Jenny to the lake.

5. She _____ her how to fish.

6. Grandma said, "I am a good teacher, Jenny,

   _____ you did catch something!"

7. But all that Jenny _____ was an old boot!

8. So Grandma and Jenny went to the store and

   _____ some fish for supper!

Harcourt Brace School Publishers

Name _____

Choose the word that matches each clue. Write the words to complete the puzzle.

bought	fault	ought	squawk
claw	fought	sauce	taught
crawl	hawk	saw	thought

ACROSS

2. an idea
6. a chicken's sound
7. had a fight
9. paid for
10. to go on hands and knees

DOWN

1. should
3. a bird
4. did teach
5. a part of a cat's paw
6. something that goes on noodles
7. blame; mistake
8. a tool used for cutting

Harcourt Brace School Publishers

Vowel Variant: / ô / *aw, au(gh), ou(gh)* • Reading Words with *aw, au(gh), ou(gh)* Phonics Practice Book

Name _____

Look at each picture. Then write the word that answers the question.

1	Has she crawled or caught it?	_____
2	Is this a paw or a paddle?	_____
3	Does it go across or under?	_____
4	Would you drink water from a bottle or a butter?	_____
5	Does he have a table or a thought?	_____
6	Is this a toaster or a turtle?	_____
7	Is this animal a fawn or a feather?	_____
8	Do you blow out a candle or a couch?	_____
9	Does a hammer or a hawk fly?	_____
10	Is she a dinner or a daughter?	_____

Review of: / ə / a, / ə l / le, / ə r / er; / ô / aw, au(gh), ou(gh)

Harcourt Brace School Publishers

Name _____

Circle the sentence that tells about the picture.

1		Julian is asleep. Julian goes away. Julian eats an apple.
2		The beaver bought a pretzel. The beaver taught the dog to gnaw. The beaver gnaws on the wood.
3		Heather is in a saddle. Heather is afloat. Heather is a skater.
4		Paul brought it to the stable. Paul has some sauce to eat. Paul drinks through a straw.
5		Dawn puts away a puzzle. Dawn steps around the pebble. Dawn saw too much paper.
6		Kate sits and uses a straw. Kate eats an apple on the lawn. Kate brought a flower ashore.

Harcourt Brace School Publishers

Review of: / ə / a, / ə l / le, / ə r / er; / ô / aw, au(gh), ou(gh)

Name _____

Circle and write the letter or letters that complete the word in each sentence.

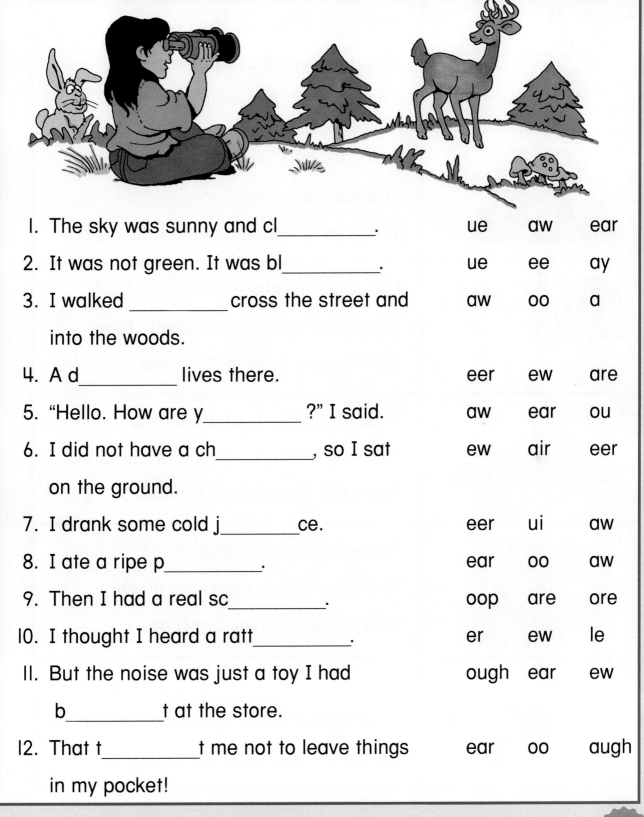

1. The sky was sunny and cl_____ .   ue   aw   ear

2. It was not green. It was bl_____ .   ue   ee   ay

3. I walked _____ cross the street and   aw   oo   a

   into the woods.

4. A d_____ lives there.   eer   ew   are

5. "Hello. How are y_____ ?" I said.   aw   ear   ou

6. I did not have a ch_____ , so I sat   ew   air   eer

   on the ground.

7. I drank some cold j_____ce.   eer   ui   aw

8. I ate a ripe p_____ .   ear   oo   aw

9. Then I had a real sc_____ .   oop   are   ore

10. I thought I heard a ratt_____ .   er   ew   le

11. But the noise was just a toy I had   ough ear   ew

    b_____ t at the store.

12. That t_____ t me not to leave things   ear   oo   augh

    in my pocket!

Harcourt Brace School Publishers

Cumulative Review: / ĭr / ear, eer; / âr / air, ear, āre; / oo / ue, u-e,
ew, oo, ou, ui; / ə / a, / əl / le, / ər / er; / ô / aw, au(gh), ou(gh)

Circle the sentence that tells about the picture.

1 	The deer will chew the apple. The deer will chase the hawk. The deer will play with the bears.
2 	The deer and fawns are in the field. The hare is eating fruit. The hare is hopping across the field.
3 	Ella found a little worm in the fruit. I thought I heard Ella's pretty tune. Ella brought food to the table.
4 	This little turtle is an awesome swimmer. This little turtle is resting on the dune. This little turtle saw a mare in the water.
5 	This youth has a hammer. This youth chooses a new flower. This youth can play the flute.
6 	My daughter rides away on the mare. My daughter blows bubbles on the stairs. My mare snoozes in the stable.

Cumulative Review: / ir / ear, eer; / âr / air, ear, are; / oo / ue, u-e, ew, oo, ou, ui; / ə / a, / əl / le, / ər / er; / ô / aw, au(gh), ou(gh)

Phonics Practice Book

Harcourt Brace School Publishers

Name _____

Fill in the circle next to the name of each picture.

1

- ○ harp
- ○ hook
- ○ hawk

2

- ○ bear
- ○ bar
- ○ board

3

- ○ fought
- ○ feared
- ○ fruit

4

- ○ paw
- ○ pear
- ○ poor

5

- ○ cool
- ○ corn
- ○ coin

6

- ○ oar
- ○ air
- ○ our

7
- ○ fear
- ○ far
- ○ four

8

- ○ stir
- ○ star
- ○ store

9

- ○ foil
- ○ fern
- ○ fawn

10

- ○ carry
- ○ cowboy
- ○ cattle

11
- ○ more
- ○ mare
- ○ moo

12
- ○ door
- ○ deer
- ○ dare

13

- ○ puzzle
- ○ pail
- ○ pearl

14

- ○ board
- ○ bird
- ○ beard

15

- ○ saddle
- ○ sadder
- ○ settle

Harcourt Brace School Publishers

Phonics Practice Book

Test: Vowel Variants

Fill in the circle next to the word that best completes each sentence.

1. We went to a country ____ .	◯ far	◯ fur	◯ fair
2. We saw a very funny ____ .	◯ clown	◯ corn	◯ coin
3. He ran ____ a horse.	◯ alone	◯ apple	◯ after
4. Then the horse ____ around.	◯ town	◯ tuned	◯ turned
5. It chased the clown ____ the tent.	◯ asleep	◯ afraid	◯ around
6. We ____ with laughter.	◯ rained	◯ roared	◯ root
7. The funny man ____ a funny hat.	◯ were	◯ wore	◯ water
8. We heard some ____ singing.	◯ birds	◯ boards	◯ bowl
9. They ____ out of his hat.	◯ flew	◯ floor	◯ flute
10. The clown's ____ was purple and green.	◯ sauce	◯ suit	◯ soup
11. It was getting ____ .	◯ dreary	◯ dart	◯ dirty
12. But the clown didn't ____ . He was having too much fun!	◯ caught	◯ core	◯ care

Test: Vowel Variants

Phonics Practice Book

Name _____

When the letter **s** is followed by a consonant at the beginning of a word, blend the sounds for the letters. Circle and write the letters that complete each word.

1. Luis will _____ art a picture.   **sc**   **st**   **sp**

2. He puts on a _____ ock.   **sm**   **sp**   **sk**

3. He paints a dog with _____ ots.   **st**   **sm**   **sp**

4. The dog is _____ art .   **sm**   **sc**   **st**

5. It paints a _____ ar!   **sp**   **sn**   **st**

6. Now Luis must _____ op.   **sk**   **st**   **sp**

7. He _____ ips outside.   **st**   **sn**   **sk**

8. And that is the end of this _____ ory! **st**   **sc**   **sm**

Name _____

Write the word that answers each question.

sky   scarf   snow   smile   small   spots   story   steps

1. What can you play in that is cold?   _____

2. What might you put on when you
   play outside?   _____

3. What can you go up or down?   _____

4. Where is the sun?   _____

5. What can you read?   _____

6. What do some cows have?   _____

7. What means "not big"?   _____

8. What do you do when you're happy?   _____

Initial Clusters with *s* • Reading Words with Clusters with *s*   Phonics Practice Book

Name _____

frog

When a consonant is followed by the letter **r** at the beginning of a word, both sounds are heard. Circle and write the letters that complete each word.

I. A mouse and a _____ og lived in a yard.   **fr   gr   cr**

2. A cat _____ om the city moved next door.   **br   tr   fr**

3. Cat wanted to catch Mouse in a _____ ap.   **pr   tr   br**

4. He _____ agged a box across the yard.   **dr   gr   fr**

5. He _____ opped some food into the box.   **gr   tr   dr**

6. Frog saw Cat and called to Mouse, "Do not   **gr   dr   cr**

_____ oss the yard today!" So Cat did not

catch Mouse.

7. Now Frog, Mouse, and Cat are _____ iends.   **fr   pr   br**

8. They all play together in the   **dr   gr   tr**

_____ een grass.

Name _____

pr   cr   gr   fr   dr   tr

1. I rhyme with *backs* and tell what animal
   feet make.   _____

2. I rhyme with *pass* and name something
   green.   _____

3. I rhyme with *log* and am a green animal
   that jumps.   _____

4. I rhyme with *less* and am something your
   mom might put on.   _____

5. I rhyme with *tab* and am an animal that
   lives in water.   _____

6. I rhyme with *top.* I tell what your books do
   when they fall.   _____

7. I rhyme with *mops.* I name plants someone
   grows for food.   _____

8. I rhyme with *mess.* I tell what you do to
   make the doorbell ring.   _____

Initial Clusters with *r* • Phonograms   Phonics Practice Book

Name _____

When a consonant is followed by the letter **l** at the beginning of a word, blend the sounds the letters stand for.

clam

Circle and write the letters that complete each word.

1. The boy watched his _____ ock of sheep.   pl   fl   **cl**

2. One of the sheep ran to the _____ iff.   **cl**   fl   bl

3. The little _____ ack sheep did not

come back.   pl   **bl**   cl

4. The boy heard a _____ ock ring out

the time.   **cl**   pl   bl

5. The boy began to _____ ink his eyes.   pl   gl   **bl**

6. Then he saw the sheep on a _____ at

rock.   **fl**   bl   cl

7. He climbed up to the sheep and said   **Pl**   Gl   Bl

"_____ ease come back."

Name _____

Write the answer to each riddle. The letters will help you.

bl fl pl cl

1. I rhyme with *tag.* I go up in the morning and down at night.

   _____

2. I rhyme with *sniff.* I am a high place made of rock.

   _____

3. I rhyme with *sink* and tell what you do with your eyes.

   _____

4. I rhyme with *sock,* and you look at me to tell time.

   _____

5. I rhyme with *cap* and am what wings do.

   _____

6. I rhyme with *ant.* I am green and I grow.

   _____

7. I rhyme with *dock,* and you can play with me.

   _____

8. I rhyme with *tap.* I tell what you can do with your hands.

   _____

Name _____

When a consonant is followed by the letter **w** at the beginning of a word, blend the sounds the letters stand for.
Write **sw** or **tw** to complete the word in each sentence.

swim

1. This morning I helped Mother _____ eep.

2. Then I went for a _____ im in the lake.

3. I saw a big _____ an that lives in the lake.

4. I saw _____ elve ducks in the lake, too.

5. There is a _____ ing in the oak tree next to the lake.

6. I have been on it _____ ice today.

7. I do not like to _____ ist around when I go up high.

8. The _____ in boys from next door are playing with me now.

9. They always trick me when they _____ itch places with one another!

Name _____

1. I rhyme with *keep.* I am something
you do when you clean.

_____

2. I rhyme with *nice* and mean
"two times."

_____

3. I rhyme with *him* and tell what
ducks do in water.

_____

4. I rhyme with *feet.* I am a sound
a bird makes.

_____

5. I rhyme with *fins.* I name two
children who look the same.

_____

6. I rhyme with *ring* and you
can ride on me.

_____

7. I rhyme with *big* and am a small
stick.

_____

8. I rhyme with *list* and mean "to
turn or bend."

_____

Name _____

1. Find the big clam. Put a small clam next to it.
2. Put a flat rock on the beach next to Swan.
3. Put a flag in the right spot on the boat.
4. Put green grass at the top of the big cliff.
5. Make a twin for the duck. Make them swim together.
6. Put a scarf around Frog's neck.
7. Add enough stars in the sky to make twelve.
8. Color the hat on Frog black.
9. Make a ring around the tracks in the sand.
10. Put an **X** on the animal with a smock.

Harcourt Brace School Publishers

Name _____

"FRAN'S NOT-SO-GREAT DAY"

The day did not get off to a good start. The bell on my clock rang twice, but I did not hear it. I had to eat my breakfast in a hurry. I did not mean to drop my drink. I got a spot on my skirt. Next, I could not find my blue scarf.

In art class, I had to swap smocks with Frank. I put green grass and a lake in the picture I made. I put a frog and a swan in my picture, too. Did I see the frog hop from the grass? Did I see the swan swim in the water? I took another look. The frog and swan were still in their same places. My eyes were playing tricks on me. I was glad when the day came to an end at last!

1. Fran's clock rang _____.

2. A _____ got on her skirt when she let her

   drink _____.

3. Fran had to give her _____ to Frank and take his.

4. Did Fran think that the _____ could hop and the

   _____ could swim?

Harcourt Brace School Publishers

Name _____

scratch

string

When the letters **scr** and **str** come together at the beginning of a word, all three sounds are heard.

Use the letters **scr** or **str** to write the word that answers each riddle.

1. I rhyme with *green.* I can go on a window. _____

2. I rhyme with *fetch.* I'm what you do when you get up. _____

3. I rhyme with *feet.* I'm what cars go on. _____

4. I rhyme with *match.* I'm what you do when you itch. _____

Write **scr** or **str** to complete the word in each sentence.

1. Eat good food to help you grow and be _____ong.

2. She will _____ap herself into the car with her seat belt.

3. Not a _____ap of food was left on the table.

4. I had to _____ub my dog in a tub.

Initial Clusters: *scr, str*   197

Name _____

1. I like to _____ out next to the lake. _____ scratch   switch   stretch

2. It is nice to be far away from the sounds of the city_____ _____ streets   greets   sleets

3. I always feed _____ of food to the ducks on the lake. _____ straps   scraps   slaps

4. They _____ for more with their loud quacks! _____ scream   stream   stem

5. Sometimes I see my dog _____ herself _____ stitch   catch   scratch

Harcourt Brace School Publishers

sprout

shrub

When the letters **spr** or **shr** come together at the beginning of a word, more than one sound is heard.
Use the letters **spr** or **shr** to write the word that answers each riddle.

1. I rhyme with *limp.* I am a small sea animal. _____

2. I rhyme with *shout.* I mean "start to grow." _____

3. I rhyme with *swing.* I am when many people plant a garden. _____

4. I rhyme with *wink.* I mean "get smaller." _____

Write **spr** or **shr** to complete the word in each sentence.

1. My pants have _____unk_____ , and now they don't fit!

2. This little sprout just _____ung_____ out of the ground.

3. I will _____ay_____ some
   water on my plants.

4. I _____ead_____
   some jam on my toast.

Harcourt Brace School Publishers

Name _____

Circle and write the word that best completes each sentence.

1. "How did you _____ your wrist?" asked Len.

    street sprain stain

2. "I fell when I _____ the seeds in my garden," said Li.

    spread shred scrod

3. "I planted my garden in the _____," he added.

    string sling spring

4. "When will the plants _____ from the ground?" asked Len.

    shout scout sprout

5. "Soon. Every day I _____ water on my garden to help it grow." said Li.

    stray spray stay

6. Will you help me plant this little green _____?" asked Li.

    stub scrub shrub

7. "It looks like a big tree that has _____," said Len.

    skunk shrunk stunk

8. "It will never grow as big as a tree," said Li with a _____.

    shrug slug sprung

Initial Clusters: *spr, shr*

Name _____

When the letters **squ** or **thr** come together at the beginning of a word, more than one sound is heard.

Use the letters **squ** and **thr** to make a word to answer each riddle. Write the word.

<u>squ</u>are

<u>thr</u>ow

1. I rhyme with **beak.** I tell the sound a mouse makes.

_____

2. I rhyme with **stone.** I tell where a king sits.

_____

3. I rhyme with **wish.** I mean "to crush something."

_____

4. I rhyme with **goat.** I am inside your mouth.

_____

Write **squ** or **thr** to complete the word in each sentence.

1. A _____ id is a sea animal.

2. It does not have _____ ee arms. It has eight!

3. It can _____ irt dark ink when it is chased.

4. This sea animal can swim _____ ough the water very fast .

Initial Clusters: *squ, thr* • Writing Words

Name_____

Circle and write the word that best completes each sentence.

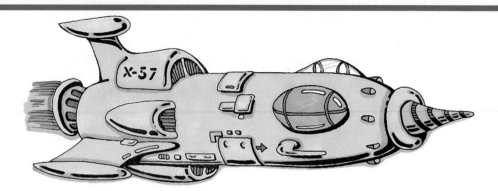

1. What a _____ it would
   be to ride in a spaceship!   shrill   quill   thrill

2. I would sit still and not
   _____ before takeoff.   squirm   cream   storm

3. Then I would hear, "_____,
   two, one! Blast off!"   spree   three   tree

4. I would be so happy that I
   would _____.   stroll   scroll   squeal

5. Could I see the ground if I were
   to _____ my eyes?   sprint   stint   squint

6. If I could _____ a ball,
   would it float or fall?   throw   crow   slow

7. I hope that one day I can fly
   _____ space.   crew   through   strap

8. I'll _____ my eyes
   closed and make a wish.   trees   breeze   squeeze

Name _____

Do what the sentences tell you.

1. Find the sea animal whose name starts like *squeak.* Color it red.
2. Draw a face on the shrimp.
3. Put a three on the third door.
4. Find the bear that will throw the ball. Color it blue.
5. Put a string at the end of the girl's kite.
6. How will the girl scrub the truck? Give her a scrub brush.
7. Color the shrub green.
8. Where is the spray from the hose? Make some spray.

Name _____

REVIEW

Read the story, and think about what happens. Then complete the sentences with words from the story.

THE SQUID AND THE SHRIMP

I had a dream that a big squid with eight arms came up on the beach. Three shrimp sat quietly on its head. "Ouch!" the squid shouted. "You scratched me! Scram!" The shrimp just gave a shrug.

The squid began to squirm to make the shrimp fall off. The shrimp were strong and did not fall. The squid said, "Get off, or I will spray water on you." The shrimp did not care.

The squid gave a shriek. "Get off, or I will throw you off," it said. The shrimp did not spring from the squid's head. They knew that the squid was not mean.

The squid asked, "Do you think my head is your throne?" The shrimp did not make a squeak.

Then I woke up and scratched the top of my head.

1. The _____ is a sea animal with eight arms.

2. There are three _____.

3. The squid began to _____, but the shrimp did not fall off.

4. That's because the shrimp were _____.

5. Why do you think the child _____ her head?

Review of Initial Clusters: *scr, str, spr, shr, squ, thr*

Phonics Practice Book

The word **slice** ends with the soft **c** sound. When the letter **c** is followed by the letter **e,** it usually stands for the soft *c* sound.

Read the poem. Then draw a picture to show what it describes.

sli<u>ce</u>

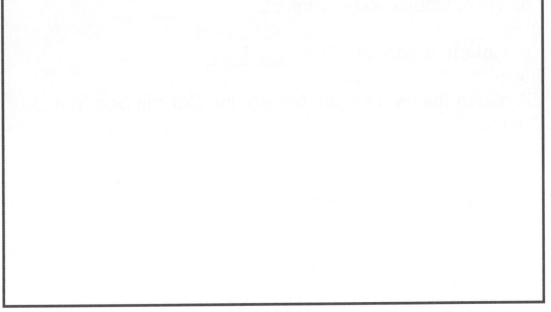

Space Mice

Two ships are going into space.

It looks as if they are in a race.

Inside the ships, I see two mice.

One of them is eating rice.

The other one is chewing ice.

Look at them, not once, but twice.

I think these mice are very nice.

Name _____

Write the word that best completes each sentence.

twice	pace	chance	race
fence	face	juice	rice

The Race

1. Cat wanted to beat Mouse in a running _____.

2. "You do not have a _____ to win," Cat said.

3. "I am _____ as fast as you."

4. Mouse laughed and made a silly _____.

5. Then, Mouse had a drink of _____.

6. Cat ate a bowl of _____.

7. When the race began, Mouse and Cat ran at a fast

   _____.

8. They both reached the _____ at the very
   same time!

Final Consonant: / s / *ce* • Reading Words

Harcourt Brace School Publishers

Phonics Practice Book

Name _____

celery   **circle**   **cymbals**

When the letter **c** is followed by the letter **e, i,** or **y,** it often stands for the soft **c** sound that you hear at the beginning of **celery, circle,** and **cymbals**. Read the sentences and circle the words that begin like **celery, circle,** or **cymbals**.

1. Today we went to the city.

2. We went to the big circus there.

3. In the center ring, a horse did tricks.

4. In the first ring, a dog rode a cycle.

5. In the third ring, a tiger jumped through a circle of fire.

6. I got a box of popcorn for 75 cents!

Write each word you circled and draw a picture for it.

1	2	3
_____	_____	_____
4	5	6
_____	_____	_____

Name _____

Write the word from the box that completes each puzzle.

> cent   cyclone   cellar   circle
> cider   city   cycle

1

A kind of bad storm is a _____.

2

A drink made from apples is _____.

3

A _____ is a place with a lot of stores.

4

A round shape is called a _____.

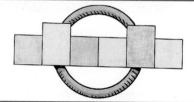

5

One _____ and nine more make 10¢.

6

A word that means "to ride a bike" is _____.

7

You go down the stairs in a house to get to the _____.

Initial Consonant: / s / *ce, ci, cy* • *Reading Words with ce, ci, cy*   Phonics Practice Book

Harcourt Brace School Publishers

Name _____

cage

badge

The words **cage** and **badge** end with the soft **g** sound. When the letter **g** is followed by the letter **e**, it usually stands for the soft **g** sound.
Circle and write the word that best completes each sentence.

1. This book has pictures of very _____ animals.	lake large lag
2. Here is a bear that is _____!	hug huge husk
3. It is by the _____ that goes over the river.	bridge bring brick
4. Look at this tiger on the rocky _____.	led ledge leg
5. What do you think is on the next _____?	page pat pane
6. It is a buffalo roaming on the _____.	rang range raise

Name _____

On the Range

Ann went out west last summer. She stayed in an old lodge. Ann had to change from her city clothes. She met a girl named Page, who was her same age.

Ann and Page went for a mule ride. Jack was in charge. He led the group to the ridge, and they looked at the open range.

On the way back to the lodge, Ann's mule would not budge. Ann tried to nudge it, but she could not urge it to move. Then, Page held out a wedge of pear. The mule made a lunge for it. Soon they were on their way again.

Use words from the story to answer the questions.

1. Where did Ann stay on her trip out West? _____

2. Whom did Ann meet that was her age? _____

3. What open space did Ann see from the ridge? _____

4. What did the mule do when it saw the wedge of pear? _____

gem

giraffe

gym

When the letter **g** is followed by the letter **e, i,** or **y**, it often stands for the soft **g** sound that you hear at the beginning of **gem, giraffe,** and **gym**. Read the story, and draw a picture of what is described in the story. Use words from the story to label your picture.

Today I met a gerbil. But it was not a small one. It was a giant one! It was as big as a giraffe! It was big, but it was gentle. The big animal said its name was Ginger. That was funny because my name is Ginger, too!

Name _____

Gene likes to take pictures. Look at the pictures from Gene's photo album. Then do what the sentences tell you.

Here I am in Georgia

1. Color the giraffe yellow.

2. Write *George* under the picture with the growling tiger.

3. Color the gerbil blue.

4. Put a large apple on the giant tree.

5. Find the girl. Write *Gina* under her picture.

6. Put a gem on the pillow in the case.

Initial Consonant: / j / *ge, gi, gy* • Reading Words in Context   Phonics Practice Book

When the letters **mb** come together at the end of a word, they stand for the sound you hear at the end of **thumb.** Look at each picture.

Write the word that makes each sentence tell about the picture.

thu<u>mb</u>

| lamb | crumb | climb | comb | limb |

1 My big, black cat likes

to _____ trees.

2 Sometimes it goes up to

a very high _____ .

3 If my cat sees a bird eating a

_____ , he comes right down.

4 I like to _____ my cat's hair.

5 Then my cat feels as soft

as a _____ .

Name _____

1. Find the stage. Put lace on the bottom of the puppet stage.
2. Find the children in a circle. Put an **X** on the child in the center.
3. Color the lamb red.
4. Color the bridge blue.
5. The girl with a bow is eating some celery. Draw the celery.
6. Put a face on the giraffe.

Review of Consonants: / s / *ce, ci, cy;* / j / *ge, dge, gi, gy;* / m / *mb*   Phonics Practice Book

Name _____

Read the story. Then, use words from the story to complete the sentences.

REVIEW

Gerry thought school was hard. Then he spent a Saturday with his dad. In the morning, they trimmed a hedge in Mr. Ginger's yard. Then Gerry's dad cut a huge limb from a giant oak tree. He had to climb on a ladder. "This is what it must feel like to be a giraffe," Dad joked. He used his saw to slice through the thick bark. The limb fell to the center of the yard with a bounce. Gerry said, "You work hard, Dad. I think I would rather be in school!"

1. Dad and _____ went to work.

2. Dad cut a huge _____ from the giant tree.

3. Dad felt like a _____ when he was on the ladder.

4. The big branch fell into the _____ of the yard.

Name _____

When the letters **lk, sk,** or **sp** are blended at the end of a word, both sounds are often heard.

Write **lk, sk,** or **sp** to complete the incomplete word in each sentence.

milk   desk   wasp

1. At the zoo Tony saw an animal with a tu_____

2. He saw a silkworm that was spinning si_____ .

3. What animal looked like it was wearing a ma_____?

4. The best was the big deer called an e_____ .

5. Tony asked the man at the de_____ to tell him about it.

6. Who do you think was drinking some cold mi_____?

Write each word you completed. Draw a picture for it.

1	2	3
_____	_____	_____

4	5	6
_____	_____	_____

Final Clusters: *lk, sk, sp* • Reading Words   Phonics Practice Book

Read the story. Then answer the questions with words from the story.

ELLIE TAKES A RISK

Ellie was an elk who wanted to see more of the world. "I will take a risk and go to the big city," Ellie said. Ellie set out at a brisk pace. The air was cool and crisp. Soon Ellie began to see houses, cars, buses, and trucks.

Then Ellie heard people gasp. A little boy wearing a mask and a silk cape came up and asked, "What kind of animal are you?"

"I'm an elk who needs something to drink," said Ellie.

"Here, have some milk," said the boy.

Ellie got back home by dusk. She sat at her desk and wrote a letter to her mother. Ellie told her mother all about the big trip!

1. What kind of animal was Ellie? _____

2. What did Ellie hear people do? _____

3. What did Ellie drink? _____

4. What time of day is just before dark? _____

5. Where did Ellie sit when she got home? _____

Name _____

belt

When a consonant is followed by the letter **t** at the end of a word, both consonant sounds are usually heard.

Write the word from the box that completes each sentence.

west	drift	knelt	toast	felt
went	raft	crust	tent	breakfast

1. Mom got down and _____ on the ground to start a fire.

2. Dad cooked a hot _____ for us over the fire.

3. We had eggs and _____ with jam on it.

4. Some birds ate the _____ of the bread.

5. Later Sam and I _____ to the lake.

6. We floated in the water on our _____ .

7. It _____ good to be on the lake on this hot, sunny day.

8. After lunch, we put up our _____ so we could sleep near the lake.

9. Later that day, we saw the sun set in the _____ .

10. Soon we would all _____ off to sleep.

Final Clusters with *t* • Reading Words

Phonics Practice Book

Name _____

Circle the best answer to each riddle.

1 You put this on over a shirt. vest vent verse volt	**2** This is not your right hand. It is your other hand. lost left lent list
3 It lives in the ground. art arm ant east	**4** This tells how something could feel. sent sort soft sat
5 Ice cubes do this in the sun. meant melt mast mint	**6** This is green and grows. plant past pelt plot
7 This is part of your arm. roast went raft wrist	**8** Birds live here. knelt nest neat neck
9 You can use this to make a picture. past paint pelt pest	**10** This can keep you warm. quit quack quilt quest

Name

Do what the sentences tell you.

1. Color the vest green.
2. Put some toast on the tray.
3. Find the raft in the picture on the wall. Color it brown.
4. Put a mask on the child with the cast.
5. Color the milk blue.
6. Color the elk red.
7. Circle the name on the list that ends like **want.**
8. Add another gift to the pile on the desk.
9. Put an ant on the book about bugs.
10. Print your name at the end of the list on the card.

Review of Final Clusters: *lk, sk, sp, st, nt, lt, ft*

Phonics Practice Book

Name _____

Read the story. Then complete the sentences with words from the story.

REVIEW

The Best Picture

Walt's school was having an art show. Walt spent a long time thinking about what to paint. He thought of a story about a silkworm. The silkworm's silk was so soft that it would melt as soon as he made it. Every day the silkworm would spin his silk to make a web. Yet, by dusk, the silk would be gone. The silkworm felt tired. Without a web, he had no place to rest.

One day, a queen came from the west. She was very nice and said, "I can make enough silk for both of us. From now on, I will share my silk with you." And she did. At last the silkworm had a web!

Walt's painting showed the two silkworms. His picture was the best!

1. Walt used _____ to make a picture.

2. The story was about a silkworm who spun _____ .

3. The silkworm had no place to _____ .

4. A queen from the _____ helped the silkworm.

Name _____

Write the word from the box that best completes each sentence.

tracks	throat	stop	city	grass	drift
flock	stretch	felt	lamb	from	vest

1. A small, green frog _____ the country was going on a train trip.

2. He had packed a blue _____.

3. The train was on its _____.

4. When it came to a _____, the frog got on.

5. The frog found a seat where he could _____ his legs.

6. Then the frog began to _____ off to sleep.

7. Two sheep and their little _____ got on the train.

8. They were going to the big _____, too.

9. The mother sheep had a sore _____.

10. She could not swallow the _____ that grew on the hill.

11. She _____ quite sick and wanted to get better.

12. Then the three sheep would go home to their _____.

Cumulative Review: Consonant Clusters, Soft *g*, Soft *c*, and *mb*   Phonics Practice Book

Name _____

Write the word from the box that answers each question.

blink	**giraffe**	**scratch**	**twice**
cent	**swim**	**cymbals**	**squeak**
shrimp	**spring**	**sponge**	**cliff**

1. What can you use to soak up spilled milk? _____

2. What can you save in a piggy bank? _____

3. What comes before summer? _____

4. What do you do in a pool? _____

5. What sound do mice make? _____

6. What lives in the sea and has a shell? _____

7. What is something people can do with their eyes? _____

8. What can you clang together to make loud sounds? _____

9. What animal has a very long neck? _____

10. What do you do when you have an itch? _____

11. What is a high, rocky place? _____

12. What means "two times"? _____

Name _____

Fill in the circle next to the name of each picture.

1	○ thumb ○ thirst ○ trust	2	○ square ○ cart ○ circle	3	○ stay ○ stray ○ spray
4	○ ant ○ ask ○ art	5	○ shock ○ stock ○ smock	6	○ crab ○ scab ○ grab
7	○ gem ○ gum ○ grim	8	○ bring ○ sting ○ string	9	○ desk ○ dent ○ deck
10	○ quit ○ quest ○ quilt	11	○ giraffe ○ gopher ○ goose	12	○ tree ○ three ○ spree

Test: Consonant Clusters, Soft *g*, Soft *c*, and *mb*

Phonics Practice Book

Name _____

1
- ○ Rabbit sits in the center of the circle.
- ○ Rabbit sits in the back of the palace.
- ○ Rabbit stands on a grassy hill.

2
- ○ Rabbit spots Frog on the grass.
- ○ Rabbit opens a gift from Frog.
- ○ Rabbit throws a ball to Frog.

3
- ○ It is a pretty vest with stripes.
- ○ It is a pretty shirt with spots.
- ○ It is a pretty silk scarf with spots.

4
- ○ Three friends run behind the fence.
- ○ The twins race to the tree.
- ○ Two shrimp rush across the tracks.

5
- ○ Frog sprains his left foot on the stump.
- ○ Squid scratches an arm on the tree.
- ○ Squid and Shrimp stay under the tree.

6
- ○ Rabbit sweeps dirt from the bridge.
- ○ Shrimp swims home under the bridge.
- ○ Shrimp drifts away on the large raft.

Name _____

The letters **ch** stand for one sound. They usually stand for the sound you hear at the beginning of **chick**. Write **chick** the word that names each picture.

| chop | chin | chair | check | children | chest |

1. _____

2. _____

3. _____

4. _____

5. _____

6. _____

Write the word from above that completes each sentence.

1. Four _____ walked by the lake.

2. They found a big _____ .

3. Tina scratched her _____ and said, "What is in it?"

4. Billy wanted to _____ inside.

5. He used a rock to _____ open the lock.

6. Inside was a doll sitting in a _____.

Name _____

The letters **ch** and **tch** usually stand for the sound you hear at the end of **peach** and **watch**. Write the word that names each picture.

pea<u>ch</u>

wa<u>tch</u>

(**branch   switch   sandwich   hatch   bench   patch**)

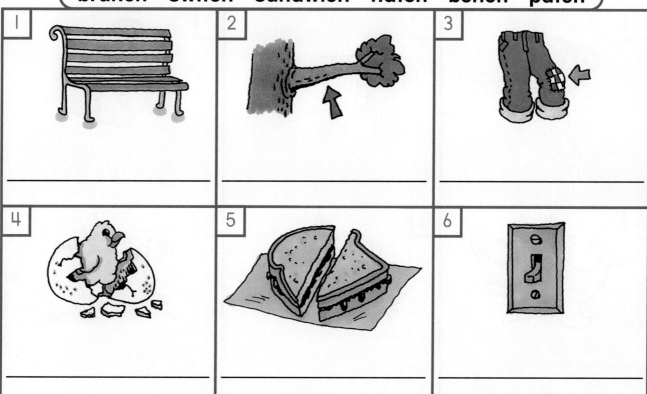

1. _____

2. _____

3. _____

4. _____

5. _____

6. _____

Circle and write the word that answers each question.

1. What do rubber bands do? _____   such   stretch   chase

2. What do grapes come in? _____   bunch   bench   brush

3. What shows you the time? _____   chick   chip   watch

4. What can you do with a mitt? _____   crutch   catch   cash

Name_____

The letters *sh* stand for one sound. They usually stand for the sound you hear at the beginning of *sheep*. Write **sheep** the word that names each picture.

shelf   shark   ship   shadow   shirt   shell

Write one of the picture names to complete each sentence.

1. My mother, my father, and I went on a _____ .

2. We saw a _____ in the water.

3. It looked like a big, dark _____.

4. I put on a _____.

5. Later I found a _____ in the sand.

6. At home, I will put it on my _____.

Initial Digraph: / sh / *sh* • Reading Words with *sh*   Phonics Practice Book

Name_____

trash   bush   brush   leash   dish   finish

| 1 | 2 | 3 |
| 4 | 5 | 6 |

Circle and write the word that answers each question.

1. What is a shark?   _____ bush   fish   chart

2. What is a loud sound? _____ crash   crutch class

3. What can children do in
   the water?   _____ such   sash   splash

4. What do you do when
   you are in a hurry?   _____ rich   rush   rash

Harcourt Brace School Publishers

Name _____

thimble

Circle and write the letter or letters that stand for the beginning sound of each picture name.

1	t th	2	t th	3	t th
4	t th	5	t th	6	t th
7	t th	8	t th	9	t th
10	t th	11	t th	12	t th

Initial Digraph: / th / *th*

Harcourt Brace School Publishers

Name _____

nor<u>th</u>

Write the word that best completes each sentence.

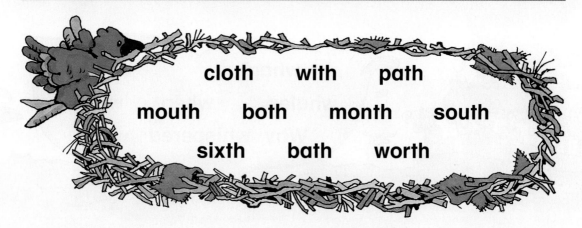

cloth   with   path

mouth   both   month   south

sixth   bath   worth

1. Some birds fly _____ in the winter.

2. Today is the _____ of March.

3. This is the _____ when some birds fly back.

4. Today I walked down a _____ .

5. I saw two birds take a _____ .

6. They _____ splashed.

7. One found some _____ .

8. What did she do _____ it?

9. She put it in her _____ to use in her nest.

10. It is _____ the long wait to see the birds in the

spring.

Harcourt Brace School Publishers

Name _____

The letters **wh** stand for the sounds that you hear at the beginning of **wheel.** Write the word that best completes **wheel** each sentence.

wharf   What

whales   when   while

Why   whispered   white

1. Mother said, "Put on your _____ shirt ."

2. Then she _____, "I have a surprise for you."

3. "_____ is it?" I asked as we got into the car.

4. "You'll find out in a _____," she said.

5. Mother went to the _____.

6. "_____ did we come here?" I asked.

7. "You will find out _____ we get on the boat," she said.

8. We went out to see _____.

Initial Digraph: / hw / wh • Reading Words with wh   Phonics Practice Book

Name _____

REVIEW

1 _____ ick	2 _____ ale	3 _____ mo
4 _____ orn	5 _____ ip	6 _____ irty
7 _____ eel	8 _____ est	9 _____ eep
10 bran _____	11 sou _____	12 fi _____

Name _____

Write the word that answers each question.

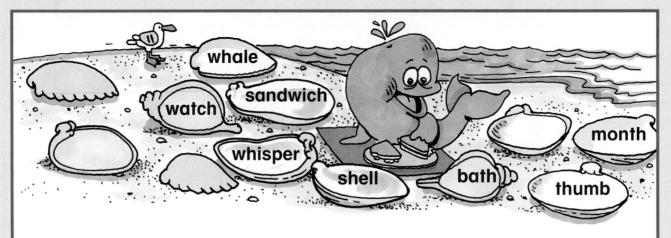

1. What is a part of your hand? _____

2. What can you take in a tub? _____

3. What lives in the sea and is
   very big? _____

4. What is May or June? _____

5. What can you use to tell time? _____

6. What does a crab live inside? _____

7. What can you eat for lunch? _____

8. How do you say something
   in a soft way? _____

Name _____

 **laugh**   The letters *gh* and *ph* often stand for the sound you hear at the end of *laugh* and the beginning of *phone*.

phone   Write the word that answers each question.

phone	alphabet	elephant	dolphin
laugh	cough	enough	photo

1. What is a picture you take called? _____

2. What animal has a trunk? _____

3. What are all the letters from
   A to *Z* called? _____

4. What do you do when you
   hear a joke? _____

5. If you don't want any more,
   how much do you have? _____

6. What animal lives in the water? _____

7. What do you do when you have
   a cold? _____

8. What do you pick up when it rings? _____

Digraph: / f / *gh, ph*   235

ring Write **ng** or **nk** to complete each picture name.
Then trace the whole word.

s**i**<u>n</u><u>k</u>

1 wi_____	2 sku_____	3 stri_____
4 ba_____	5 swi_____	6 wi_____
7 spri_____	8 ki_____	9 tru_____
10 i_____	11 sli_____	12 ho_____

Name _____

 knight

gnat

Choose the word that matches each clue. Write the word to complete the puzzle.

gnaw   knife   wrench   knight   knee   wrong
wrap   wren   knock   write   gnat   knob

ACROSS

1. You turn this to open a door.
2. This rhymes with *then*. It can fly.
6. This can cut.
7. Mice do this to food.
9. You do this with a pen.
10. You can fix things with this.

DOWN

1. You make this sound on a door.
3. This is where your leg bends.
4. He works for a king.
5. This is what you do to a gift.
7. This is a small bug.
8. This means "not right."

Name _____

Circle and write the word that completes each sentence.

1. Here is a book about   gnats   knots   wraps

    _____ and other bugs.

2. This picture shows the leg   king   photo   knee

    and tells how the _____ bends.

3. This book is about a _____ .   knit   drop   dolphin

4. It takes place in the _____ .   wrist   spring   skunk

5. It makes me _____   laugh   long   link

    because it is fun to read.

6. Someday I will _____ a   phone   write   knight

    book about animals.

7. I _____ books are great!   thing   tough   think

Review of Digraphs: / f / *ph, gh;* / ng / *ng;* / ngk / *nk;* / r / *wr;* / n / *kn, gn*   Phonics Practice Book

Do what the sentences tell you.

1. Make an **X** on the knight who is looking at the elephant shield.

2. Find the door with no knob. Put a knob on it.

3. Circle any letters of the alphabet that you see.

4. Add more flowers to the wreath.

5. Put an **H** on the horse that is in the wrong place.

6. Put more leaves on the tree that is being gnawed.

7. Put a watch around the king's wrist.

8. Put a box around each knife on the table.

9. Make a check mark on the rough road.

10. Put an **X** on the skunk.

Phonics Practice Book   Review of Digraphs: / f / *ph, gh*; / ng / *ng*; / ngk / *nk*; / r / *wr*; / n / *kn, gn*

Name _____

Circle and write the letters that complete each word. Then trace the whole word.

1	ch sh gn	___ark
2	gn wr ph	___at
3	th sh ph	___one
4	th sh tch	pa___
5	nk gh ng	wi___
6	sh wh wr	___eel
7	th ch sh	___eese
8	ph th ch	ele___ant
9	ch wr kn	___ight
10	ph wh wr	___ist
11	ng nk gh	ba___
12	tch sh ph	swi___

Cumulative Review: Digraphs

Phonics Practice Book

Harcourt Brace School Publishers

Name _____

Read the story. Then write the word from the story that completes each sentence.

The Shell

Frank and Ruth were sitting on a bench playing chess. A little boy came up. "Look at the shell that I found at the beach," he said. "When you put this shell next to your ear, you can hear the sounds of the sea. You can hear the song of dolphins and the water crash on the sand."

Frank took the shell and put it next to his ear. He could hear the thunder of the water. Then Ruth listened. "If I close my eyes, I can picture the wharf!" she said with a laugh. "Thank you for sharing your shell with us."

1. Ruth and Frank were playing _____.

2. A boy had found a _____ at the beach.

3. The boy could hear the _____ sing when he

listened.

4. Ruth could picture the _____.

Harcourt Brace School Publishers

CHECK-UP

Fill in the circle next to the name of each picture.

1		2		3	
	○ thrill ○ chill ○ shell		○ thorn ○ torn ○ wren		○ chick ○ gopher ○ gnat

4		5		6	
	○ check ○ wreck ○ shock		○ dolphin ○ dish ○ ditch		○ match ○ much ○ moth

7		8		9	
	○ wrong ○ wreath ○ wring		○ swish ○ sink ○ swing		○ hatch ○ hang ○ honk

10		11		12	
	○ that ○ chat ○ gnat		○ bench ○ bank ○ brush		○ skunk ○ sketch ○ sting

Test: Consonant Digraphs

Name _____

Fill in the circle next to the sentence that tells about the picture.

CHECK-UP

1	
ABCDE FG 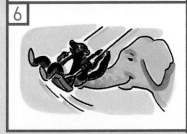	◯ Elephant writes the alphabet with chalk. ◯ Elephant writes her name with ink. ◯ Elephant writes on a graph.
2	◯ Elephant swings her trunk and laughs. ◯ Skunk taps his knees and sings. ◯ Gopher whispers something to Elephant.
3	◯ Wren shows a photo in a book. ◯ Wren brushes a moth from the table. ◯ Wren shows what month it is.
4	◯ Skunk sees a dolphin and a shark. ◯ Skunk swims in the fish tank. ◯ Skunk eats lunch now.
5	◯ Gopher cuts her sandwich with a knife. ◯ Gopher gnaws his food. ◯ Gopher and Wren both take a drink.
6	◯ Elephant climbs down from a rough branch. ◯ Elephant plays with a bunch of chicks. ◯ Elephant pushes Skunk on the swing.

Name _____

A **contraction** stands for two words. An **apostrophe** takes the place of the letter or letters that were left out.
Write the contraction for the two words below each sentence.

she + is = she's

1. _____ not very big.
       I am

2. Look at my ears. _____ big!
                   They are

3. Do you see my tail? _____ round.
                It is

4. Move the way I do. _____ hopping!
              You are

5. _____ hop away together.
       Let us

6. _____ going to have fun!
       We are

Draw a picture of the animal who is talking.

Contractions: 'm, 're, 's • Reading Contractions

Phonics Practice Book

Name_____

What Can You Find?

If you look with care,
You'll find all five.
I'll give you a clue.
One of them is *I've*.
I won't say any more.
So you'd better start looking.
Are your eyes wide open?
Now circle all five!

Write each contraction you circled next to the words it stands for.

1. I have   _____

2. you will   _____

3. will not   _____

4. you would   _____

5. I will   _____

Fill in the circle next to the contraction that stands for the underlined words.

1. I <u>can not</u> wait until Grandma comes.	○ haven't ○ can't ○ don't
2. <u>She will</u> be here soon.	○ She'd ○ She'll ○ She's
3. <u>It is</u> her birthday.	○ I'm ○ It'll ○ It's
4. <u>We are</u> having a surprise party for her.	○ We'll ○ We're ○ We've
5. <u>I have</u> made her a big birthday cake.	○ I'd ○ I'll ○ I've
6. <u>Let us</u> go out and wait for Grandma.	○ I'll ○ He's ○ Let's
7. <u>We will</u> hide and yell "Surprise."	○ We've ○ We'll ○ We'd

Test: Contractions

Phonics Practice Book

Name _____

the dog's bone

Change the underlined words in each sentence to a word that has **'s.**

---

1 | The book that <u>belongs to my sister</u> is about sea life.

My _____ book is about sea life.

---

2 | The glasses <u>that belong to my father</u> are broken.

My _____ glasses are broken.

---

3 | Here are some photos of pets <u>that belong to my friend.</u>
Here are some photos of my

_____ pets.

---

4 | The scarf <u>that belongs to my mother</u> matches her hat.

My _____ scarf matches her hat.

---

5 | The horse <u>that belongs to my sister</u> has a long tail.

My _____ horse has a long tail.

---

6 | The <u>toy that belongs to my dog</u> is flat.

My _____ toy is flat.

Harcourt Brace School Publishers

Phonics Practice Book

Possessive: 's

The word **birds'** shows that the cage belongs to the two birds. Change the underlined words in each sentence to a word that has **s'**.

1. These cats <u>belong to my sisters</u>.

   They are my _____ cats.

2. That dog <u>belongs to the boys</u>.

   It is the _____ dog.

3. These birds <u>belong to my parents</u>.

   These are my _____ birds.

4. That snake <u>belongs to my brothers</u>.

   It is my _____ snake.

5. These mice <u>belong to my friends</u>.

   They are my _____ mice.

6. These toys <u>belong to all the pets</u> that live on my street.

   These are all of the _____ toys.

Possessive: *s'*

Name _____

Write the correct word with **'s** or **s'** to complete each label.

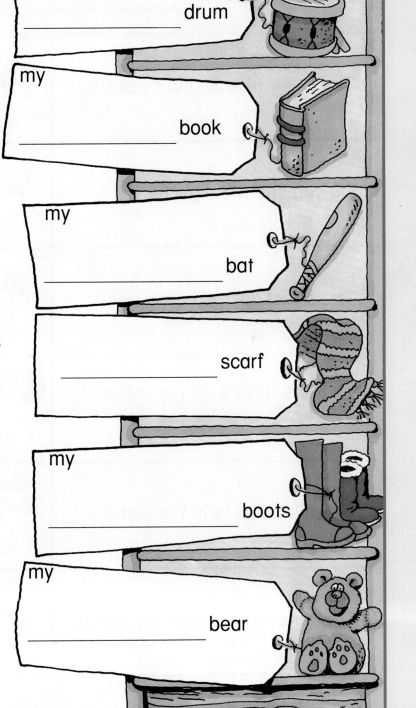

1. the drum that belongs to the baby

the _____ drum

2. the book that belongs to my sisters

my _____ book

3. the bat that belongs to my friends

my _____ bat

4. the scarf that belongs to Mom

_____ scarf

5. the boots that belong to my brothers

my _____ boots

6. the bear that belongs to my father

my _____ bear

Name _____

Read each sentence. Fill in the circle under the picture that shows who has something.

1. The bees' hive is a busy place.	○	○	○
2. Do you see the pig's pen?	○	○	○
3. The birds' nest is in the tree.	○	○	○
4. There is a fox's den in these woods.	○	○	○
5. A fish's home is in the water.	○	○	○
6. The girls' house is on my street.	○	○	○

Harcourt Brace School Publishers

Test: Possessives

Phonics Practice Book

Fill in the circle next to the sentence that tells about the picture.

1

○ The girl's toys are under the couch.
○ The girls' toys are under the couch.
○ The girls are under the couch.

2

○ The clown's hats are on.
○ The clowns' hats are on.
○ The clowns' hats are off.

3

○ My mother's socks are not on her feet.
○ My mother's socks are on her feet.
○ My mothers' socks are not on their feet.

4

○ The hens' chicks are hatching.
○ The hen's chicks are hatching.
○ The hens are watching the chicks.

5

○ The grandmothers' cats sleep.
○ The grandmother's cats sleep.
○ The grandmothers sleep.

6

○ The boy looks for his dog's bone.
○ The boy looks for his dogs' bone.
○ The boy looks for his dog.

Name _____

Replace the words below each sentence with a word that ends with **-ful** or **-ly**. Write the word.

1. Dad likes to cook, so he makes dinner _____.
   in a glad way

2. Dad chops the food _____.
   in a quick way

3. He is _____ when he uses the sharp knife.
   full of care

4. Soon he has chopped a _____ of food.
   enough to fill a pot

5. The stew cooks _____ on the stove.
   in a slow way

6. Everyone is _____ when the stew is done.
   full of cheer

7. Dinner tastes _____ !
   full of wonder

Suffixes: *-ful, -ly*

Phonics Practice Book

Name _____

In many words that end with **y,** change the **y** to **i** before adding **-es** or **-ed.**

Add the ending to the word to complete each sentence. Then write the new word.

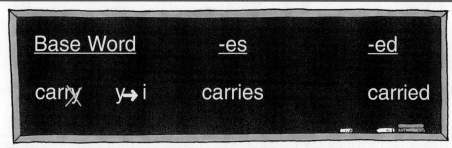

Base Word	-es	-ed
carry y→i	carries	carried

1. Alana _____ home.
   hurry + ed

2. She _____ a large box.
   carry + ed

3. There were soft _____ coming from it.
   cry + es

4. That's because there were _____ in it.
   puppy + es

5. In all, the _____ had eight legs and four ears.
   baby + es

6. Alana's friend _____ to use the clue to tell
   try + ed

   how many little dogs were in the box.

Draw a picture to show how many little dogs were in the box.

Name _____

Change **f** to **v** before adding **-es** or **-s**.

Change each underlined word to make it mean "more than one."
Write the word to complete each problem. Answer the problem.

wolf   **wol<u>ves</u>**   **knife**   **kni<u>ves</u>**

1. You have one <u>loaf</u> of bread. You get one more. How many

   _____ do you have? _____

2. Four _____ are eating. One <u>wolf</u> walks away.

   How many are left? _____

3. You eat one <u>half</u> of an apple. You eat one half more. How

   many _____ do you eat? _____

4. Five _____ are in the field. One <u>calf</u> joins

   them. How many are in the field now? _____

5. Six _____ are on the table. I take one <u>knife</u>

   away. How many are left on the table? _____

6. I found one <u>leaf</u>. My friend found nine more. How many

   _____ do we have? _____

Inflected Ending: *-es* (change *f* to *v*) • Writing Words with *es*   Phonics Practice Book

Name _____

In many words that end with a short vowel and a consonant, you double the consonant before adding **-ed** or **-ing**.

Choose the word that tells about each picture. Add **-ed** or **-ing**, and write the new word to complete the pair of sentences.

BASE WORD		-ED	-ING
HOP	+P	HOPPED	HOPPING
HUM	+M	HUMMED	HUMMING

set   hop   wag   nap   dig   scrub

1. I make a big hole. I am

_____.

2. I got dirty. Mai Ling

_____

me.

3. I got tired and sleepy.

I _____.

4. Now I am playing. I am

_____

on two legs.

5. I liked playing. I

_____

my tail.

6. The day is over. The sun is

_____.

Inflected Endings: *-ed, -ing* (double final consonant)
• Reading Words with *-ed, -ing*

Name _____

In most words that end with **e**, you drop the **e** before adding **-ed** or **-ing**.

Add **-ed** or **-ing** to the word under each sentence. Write the new word to complete the sentence.

Base Word	-ed	-ing
bake	baked	baking
hope	hoped	hoping

1. The sun is _____ in the sky.
   rise

2. Outside, small animals are just _____ up.
   wake

3. I have always _____ mornings like this.
   love

4. Everybody walks around _____.
   smile

5. My friend just _____ next door to me.
   move

6. Will and I were _____ our bikes at the beach.
   ride

7. We stopped and _____ in the water.
   wade

8. A fish jumped up and _____ us!
   surprise

Inflected Endings: *-ed, -ing* (drop final *e*)

Phonics Practice Book

Name _____

I like to watch

I like to watch the bunnies
Hopping from here to there.
They are hoping to find some carrots
That all of them can share.

I like to watch the calves
That I spotted over there.
They are standing very quietly
And enjoying the fresh air.

I like to watch the ponies
Racing in the sun.
They are running very quickly
And having a lot of fun!

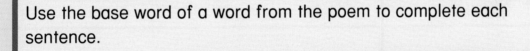

Use the base word of a word from the poem to complete each sentence.

1. The bunnies _____ from here to there.

2. They _____ to find carrots.

3. More than one _____ is standing quietly.

4. The ponies _____ in the sun.

5. They run in a _____ way.

6. They _____ a lot of fun.

Circle the sentence that tells about the picture.

1 	The wolves carried a bagful of food. The wolf carried a handful of food. The wolves saw a wolf running quickly.
2 	The playful puppies are jumping in. The playful puppies are running and hiding. The playful puppy is swimming.
3 	The pig smiled gladly and raked leaves. The pig chased a falling leaf. The pig jumped joyfully into the leaves.
4 	The frog shared a loaf of bread. The frog baked loaves of bread. The frog carried a loaf to the table.
5 	The mother is giving a mouthful to her babies. The mother is giving a potful to her baby. The mother is sharing a nest with one baby.

Cumulative Review: Inflected Endings and Suffixes

Phonics Practice Book

Name _____

Write the base word for each word.

1 gladly	2 hoped	3 carried
_____	_____	_____
4 living	5 careful	6 digging
_____	_____	_____
7 tries	8 calves	9 clapped
_____	_____	_____
10 waking	11 getting	12 puppies
_____	_____	_____

Name _____

Fill in the circle next to the word that completes each sentence.

1	Our dog Beans had three beautiful _____ six weeks ago.	○ puppy ○ puppies ○ puppy's
2	Last night I could not sleep because they _____ a lot.	○ crying ○ cries ○ cried
3	I _____ to take a nap this morning, but they climbed all over me.	○ tried ○ trying ○ tries
4	Then they jumped up and ate two _____ of freshly baked bread.	○ loaf ○ leaves ○ loaves
5	Be _____ when you pick up that spotted one.	○ careful ○ care ○ cared
6	It is the one that is _____ its tail.	○ wagged ○ wag ○ wagging
7	We _____ all the baby dogs.	○ loving ○ love ○ loves
8	We are _____ to find homes for them quickly.	○ hoping ○ hopping ○ hoped

Inflected Endings and Suffixes Test

Phonics Practice Book

Popcorn!

"Mmm, popcorn!" said Jen. "I like lots of popcorn. Let me pop some more."

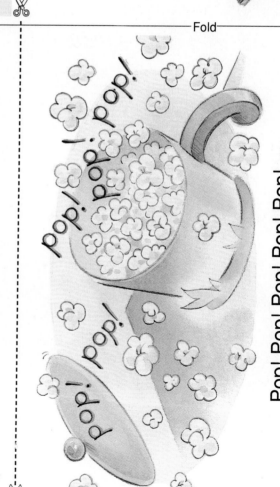

---Fold---

Fold

Harcourt Brace School Publishers

"Come have popcorn, Ben," said Red and Jen and Ted. "MMMMM, POPCORN!"

8

Pop! Pop! Pop! Pop! Pop! pop! pop! pop! pop! pop! pop!
"It will not stop," said Red. "What can we do?" said Ted.

9

Directions: Help your child cut and fold the book.
Phonics Practice Book

Cut-Out Fold-Up Book I • Short *o* Short *e*

261

"I have a pot. I will let it get hot.
Popcorn will pop. Mmm, popcorn!"
said Red.

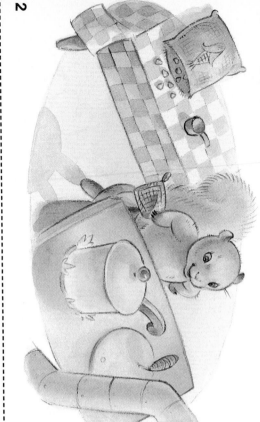

"Mmm, popcorn!" said Ted.
"It's not hot yet. I will drop some in.
It will pop and pop."

Harcourt Brace School Publishers

Fold

Fold

"Get the pot!" said Red.
"Get a mop!" said Ted.
"Get help!" said Jen.

Pop! Pop! Pop!
"The pot is hot," said Red.
"Come get popcorn."

Cut-Out Fold-Up Book I • Short *o* Short *e*

Directions: Help your child cut and fold the book.
Phonics Practice Book

Tag and the Bug

— 1

Snap! Tag snaps at the bug.
The bug gets away. It goes up.
Tag will get that bug.

3

---Fold---

---Fold---

The bug is in here. Tag taps it.
He hits it. He rips it up.
Still no bug.

6

Tag snaps at the bug. What happens?

_____

Directions: Help your child cut and fold the book.
Phonics Practice Book

Cut-Out Fold-Up Book 2 • Short *a*, Short *i*, Short *u*

Crash! Tag does not get the bug. The bug lands on the lamp. Tag still wants that bug.

The bug goes up and up.
It sees a hill.
It does not see the pup.

Fold

Fold

"Stop, Tag," says Mom. "What a mess! Out you go, bad dog." Tag goes out. So does the bug.

Tag jumps. The lamp tips and falls. The bug falls to the rug. Tag will get that bug.

7

Cut-Out Fold-Up Book 2 • Short *a*, Short *i*, Short *u*

Directions: Help your child cut and fold the book.

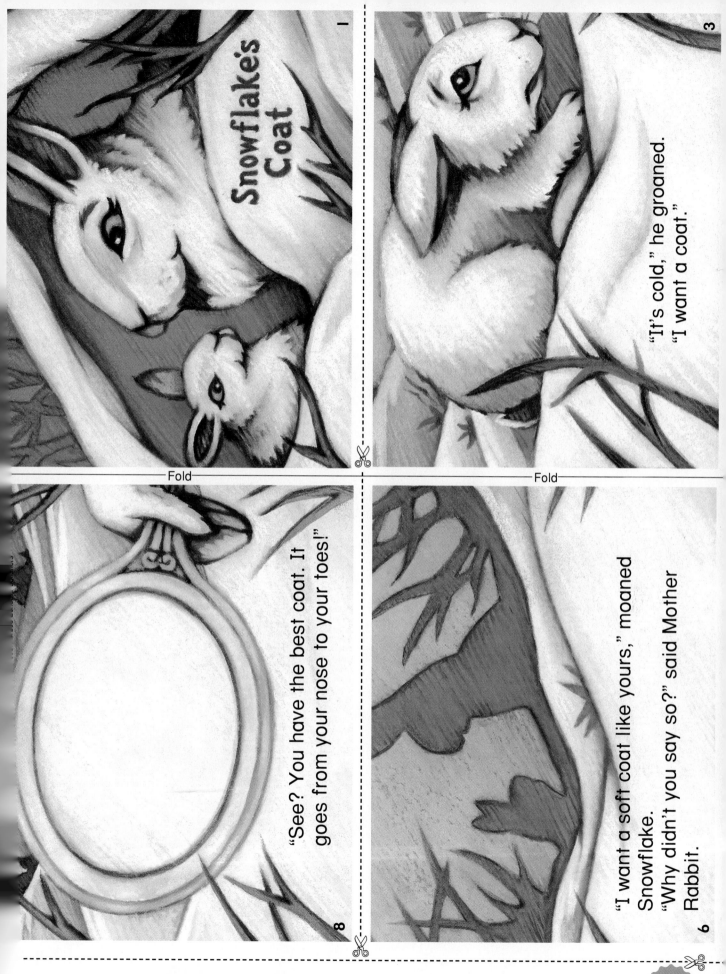

Snowflake's Coat

1

"It's cold," he groaned.
"I want a coat."

3

"See? You have the best coat. It goes from your nose to your toes!"

8

"I want a soft coat like yours," moaned Snowflake.
"Why didn't you say so?" said Mother Rabbit.

6

Directions: Help your child cut and fold the book.
Phonics Practice Book

Cut-Out Fold-Up Book 3 • Long *a*, Long *o*

265

Mother Rabbit made a coat for Snowflake. "Here, slip it on."

Fold

Mother Rabbit made a hole in the snow.
"Come, Snowflake, let's play."

Fold

"This is too much coat," Snowflake said.
"You'll grow," said Mother Rabbit.

Mother Rabbit got something from a box.
"This coat has toes and a tail," she said.

Fold - Up Book 3

Directions: Help your child cut and fold the book.
Phonics Practice Book

The Bike Ride

---Fold---

Sheep said, "I need to rest. Let's sit next to this tree. It has pretty green leaves."

3

---Fold---

. . . Mule woke up. It was night. He put on the light. It had been a dream!

8

"Buzz, buzz. What do we see next to our fine tree?" said the bees.

6

Directions: Help your child cut and fold the book.

"Will you have a peach?" asked Mule.
"Yes, please. We can have tea, too," said Sheep.

Sheep and Mule went on a bike ride.
They rode for five miles.

—Fold—

—Fold—

While Sheep ate, Mule jumped up.
"I see a big hive," said Mule.

The bees dived down.
Mule and Sheep ran in fright.
Then . . .

268 Cut-Out Fold-Up Book 4 • Long *i*, Long *e*, Long *u*

Directions: Help your child cut and fold the book.

What are sharks like? Read to find out.

-Fold-

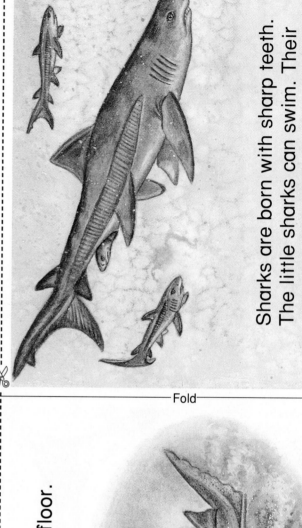

Sharks are born with sharp teeth. The little sharks can swim. Their mothers do not take care of them!

-Fold-

Sharks can live near and far from shore. They get air from the sea. That is because sharks are fish!

8

Nurse sharks live on the sea floor. Carpet sharks do, too.

9

Some little sharks grow in "mermaid's purses." They grow inside these purses the way birds grow inside eggs.

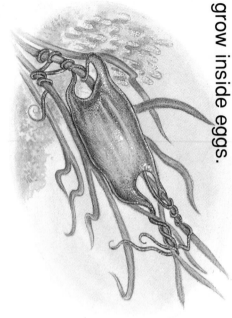

Some sharks will harm you. Other sharks will not.

Fold

You can see that sharks have sharp teeth. But you can not see their ears. The ears are inside.

Fold

The whale shark is so big that it might scare you. But do not fear! It will not hurt you.

270

Cut-Out Fold-Up Book 5 • R-Controlled Vowels

Directions: Help your child cut and fold the book.

1

A RIDDLE

3

I was round. I grew from the ground. My roots grew down for food. I grew and stood tall.

I gave you good clues. I taught you, too. Now draw me. Then show everyone what you drew!

I can be in a small group or in a big crowd, but I do not make a sound!

Would you like to play a game? I will give you clues. Then you should know what I am!

Sometimes I am on a tree before the fruit grows.

I ought to make you smile, not frown. I can be a joy to see.

I can be brought inside. You can see me in a book or in a room.

Fold

Fold

7

5

Cut-Out Fold-Up Book 6 • Vowel Variants

Directions: Help your child cut and fold the book.